PLANETARY HARMONIES

.

# PLANETARY HARMONIES

*Joan Hodgson*

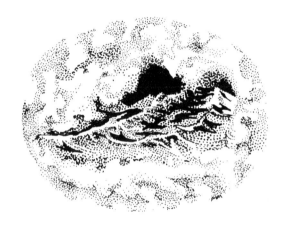

*AN ASTROLOGICAL BOOK OF MEDITATION*

*Illustrated by Margaret Clarke*

## THE WHITE EAGLE PUBLISHING TRUST

LISS · HAMPSHIRE · ENGLAND

First published October 1980
© Joan Hodgson, 1980

**British Library Cataloguing in Publication Data**

Hodgson, Joan
    Planetary harmonies.
    1. Meditation
    2. Astrology
    I. Title
    133.5        BF1729.M/
    ISBN 0-85487-047-4

*Set in 11 on 13 pt Lasercomp Baskerville*
*at Richard Clay (The Chaucer Press) Ltd, Bungay, Suffolk*
*and printed in Great Britain by*
*Fletcher & Son Ltd, Norwich*

# Contents

# I

# *The Way of Meditation*

For just over fifty years the teacher White Eagle has been showing his students how to discover within themselves the quiet places of the spirit, where in meditation they can not only find the soul-strength to cope with the problems of their own lives, but project spiritual healing to others, healing which reaches to the stresses and inharmonies in the soul which finally manifest in physical 'dis-ease'. Early in 1936, under the direction of White Eagle, the White Eagle Lodge in London came into being. It was to be a centre of peace and soul-healing, a spiritual home where people, exhausted by life's problems, could receive spiritual refreshment, strength and enlightenment. From the earliest days members were trained in White Eagle's method of thought-control and the projection of their soul-power to help the world. The Lodge was called 'a church of the New Age', for White Eagle's teachings are intended to help people respond not only to the superficial mental quickening of the Aquarian Age, but to unfold the deeper power of the living God which is locked in the heart of every man.

Although Aquarius, a sign of the air element, is quickening the mental 'body' of humanity, the influence of the opposite sign is to be felt at the same time. The polar opposite of Aquarius is the fiery Leo, sign of the Sun, which rules the heart-centre of mankind. In all his teachings through the years White Eagle has emphasised the need for man to learn how to still the busy, frontal mind and regularly withdraw into the quiet temple of the spirit. Within the heart of every one of us lies a centre of stillness and peace, a place of silence where the soul can contact God. White Eagle calls this centre of consciousness the 'mind in the heart', and its development is of vital importance as mankind comes under the developing mental pressure of the Aquarian Age. As he learns how to use it man discovers a new centre of wisdom which will bring strength and give guidance.

Just as the outer life of humanity falls into a cyclic pattern through the rhythm of day, week, month and season, man's inner life responds subtly to these changing conditions. In the Lodge, people who use their inner powers in services of religion and healing have gradually become aware of subtle differences in the psychic vibrations during the different months of the year, and more particularly at the time of the full moons. We have noticed that White Eagle's teaching given during the same month of different years often emphasises the same aspect of spiritual work, so much so that those of us responsible for preparing readings for the different services in his Lodge now almost automatically search among teachings given at about the same time of the year, when the Sun was passing through the same sign of the zodiac. These particular teachings seem to 'come alive' in a remarkable way.

As an astrological consultant I began to observe this linking of the teaching with the inner response with great interest. It confirmed my growing conviction that in order really to understand a soul one must somehow learn to merge into the planetary ray on which that soul is unfolding. Interpretation of the signs and planets was becoming for me far more a question of being and feeling in my heart than thinking and remembering with my mind. I began to be aware at the full moons of the psychic power of the prevailing signs to colour my meditation and open fresh avenues of inspiration and awareness on the soul-plane.

A favourite book, THE TEACHINGS OF THE ESSENES FROM ENOCH TO THE DEAD SEA SCROLLS, by Edmond Szekely*, made me recognise the importance of the planetary rhythm of the days of the week as a progressive force in meditation. Like the ancient Persians and Babylonians, the Essene Brotherhood at the time of the birth of Christ were deeply aware of the need for man to learn to work consciously with angels, the angels of the planets and of the elements. They believed that with this knowledge the soul of man could attain its full human and divine stature. In our terms, the Christ in man would command the elements both of his being and of the natural world. For some time I tried to follow the pattern of meditation given for the Essenes in the Dead Sea Scrolls, but being an astrologer I began to find that my response to the planetary rulers, the angels of the days of the week, was becoming important and helpful to me.

If in meditation I could manage to put myself into that planetary stream of consciousness it seemed to have the effect of putting life into the whole day, especially on those days which harmonised with my own horoscope. There is now no doubt in my mind that each day of the week comes under the influence of a planetary angel, and that if we can train ourselves to respond to these planetary harmonies an increasing richness of spiritual experience will be found. It is for this reason that I have tried to express the symbols and concepts of the planetary angels, hoping that they may prove helpful to others following the path of meditation. These are not meant to be definitions but ideas which may quicken further response in the soul as deeper understanding of the planetary ray develops.

In time I think that we will begin to realise that angels are not remote from our human concerns and that we can

* C. W. Daniel, 1957.

call upon them for strength, protection and inspiration; that it is part of the great plan that eventually men and angels will work in conscious co-operation, each evolutionary lifestream contributing to the other. The angels help man to create and use his subtler bodies. Healers at the White Eagle Lodge are taught how to invoke the help of angels. Man contributes to the life of the angels because they respond to human love and kindness and thus the healing work is helpful to both.

Perhaps the circumstance that causes most people to seek heavenly consolation is the physical death of someone close and dear. The deep yearning which follows bereavement gives a soul the impetus to search for inner light and understanding. The accumulation of remarkable evidence of personal survival after death which can be found in Spiritualist literature can be a valuable starting-point for those seeking comfort. People who are fortunate enough may receive personal evidence which at the time seems remarkable. The trouble is that the memory of this fades, and after a time they are again hungry for the spiritual contact. One cannot for ever be running to a medium.

The quiet sanctuary of the heart, to which White Eagle has tried to take us, is also the place where we can hold true spiritual communion with those we love. If we believe that although they have lost the physical body they are still very much alive in their body of light, it is logical that once we can stimulate and learn to function in our own body of light there need be no separation. By the practice of meditation we learn to bring into operation the mind of the spirit. We can train ourselves to build a bridge of light between the outer and the inner world which can heal the sting of death and parting and bring a deeper peace and happiness than the soul has known before. This is something Jesus was trying to help his disciples to

4

understand when he said, *It is expedient for you that I go away: for if I go not away, the Comforter will not come unto you; but if I depart, I will send him unto you.* When a deep love exists between two souls, the passing of one into the higher life can become for the other like the opening of a door to heavenly light and understanding, to the incoming of the Comforter. It means firm discipline of the thoughts, putting aside personal grief; and it needs a childlike approach.

The unfoldment of the inner consciousness is a slow process requiring patience and soul-effort. One might almost liken it to learning to play a musical instrument. Regular and often frustrating practice is required before the results can be really satisfying. Yet like musical accomplishment it is a supremely worthwhile effort which can lead to an ever-increasing sense of inner peace and confidence in the plan and pattern which is being worked out in every life.

The planetary meditations in this book are only given as ideas or guidelines which can quicken further response in the soul as understanding of the planetary ray unfolds.

# 2
## *Thought-Control*

Astrology gives us certain ancient symbols which form the basis of all meditation, for they are symbols of life itself and contain the story of man's destiny. In meditation they can become living emblems of the deity, its incarnation in the flesh, its immortalisation of the flesh.

Although thinking of these symbols with the outer mind can produce many interesting philosophical ideas, we have to remember that thinking is not true meditation. Meditation can only begin when the mind has been stilled, the body relaxed, and the whole being is focused peacefully on a symbol.

The first and most ancient symbol is the circle with a dot in the centre. This astrological glyph for the sun represents much more than just the solar orb in the heavens. Perhaps we should say that the dot represents the beginning, the Word, the life, the light which is the origin of creation. The circle is the great spiritual sun behind its physical counterpart, and the dot is the divine energy, the flame in the heart of every man, the nucleus of every cell. It is symbolised in eastern philosophy in the OM, the sound which vibrates through all created things.

In spiritual philosophy the dot represents not only the Sun but also the Pole Star, that great magnetic centre to which the north pole of the earth points as it spins on its axis.

Students are sometimes confused about the difference in symbolic meaning of the sun and the Pole Star, Polaris. Followers of the White Eagle teachings are taught from the very beginning to meditate on the star, yet in their absent healing groups they begin their invocation with the words, 'The ancients saw and worshipped the sun as a sign and symbol of God'. We might say that the sun is also a star, so that when we focus our meditation on the star, we are also meditating on the sun. There is however a subtle difference which will gradually become clearer as we practise deep meditation.

Both the sun and Polaris are stars. We belong to the sun's system, we are part of the life of the sun, but Polaris shines above the poles of the earth and represents the earth's own polarisation not only with the sun, but with the vast cosmos. It is the pole of the heavens.

Polaris thus signifies for man his own personal alignment with the central power of the cosmos, the great OM of eastern philosophy. It represents man's essential self, lord of his being, the individuality. We are all children of the sun, the glorious light of the heaven from which we draw strength and vitality, food for body, soul and spirit. We worship the sun as the great father of our being, but the Pole Star is the guiding principle, the summit of our aspiration, the lord of the ray on which we are evolving.

The position of the Sun in the individual horoscope shows what aspect of the solar body we have come into incarnation to build through earthly experience. It is through meditation on the glory and beauty of the sun that we come gradually to the realisation of the sun in our innermost being, recognise our own Pole Star. The man made perfect has found this sun-centre and so has made one the universal and the individual suns.

It is interesting that in the old numerology the numbers one and four were both assigned to the Sun. Since the rediscovery of Uranus, four has been assigned to him. We might almost say that Uranus, which represents man made perfect, is the planet of the fully polarised man—

the man with the fully developed solar body who is also master of his own ray of being.

If we were looking down from the Pole Star, we should see the earth revolving round the sun always with one side in darkness and one in the light. We should also see the moon revolving round the earth, again with its alternating phases of light and darkness. When we can raise our consciousness through meditation we gain a similar perspective on the problems of our earthly life. We become aware of the interplay of light and darkness and its purpose in the building of the soul-temple which in astrology is symbolised by the Moon.

Ancient wisdom teaches that the two forces of light and darkness both have an important part to play in the human soul. This idea will be familiar to students of yoga who gradually learn how to balance within themselves the lifestreams of the sun and the moon, the sun of course being positive or light, the moon negative or dark.

It is perhaps natural to associate light with goodness and darkness with evil, yet White Eagle's account of these two forces is rather different. He relates the sun lifestream to the outer life, to that part of us which is active and in control during the daylight or waking hours. The sun vitalises every part of our being, and more especially gives light and vitality to the physical body until the solar body, the body of light, can fully manifest through it.

The lunar lifestream or the dark self White Eagle relates to the invisible part of our being, which becomes more active during the hours of darkness when the conscious self is at rest; the subconscious and superconscious mind. Astrologically, too, this inner soul-life of the personality is linked with the Moon.

In ancient wisdom the moon always symbolised the soul, that deep inner part of man's being where dwell the memories of past lives, past fears, past thought-habits and past triumphs. This shadow side of man may almost be likened to a deep sea from which life emerges, an eternal source from which the outer personality draws its strength. It constitutes the inner world, into which we withdraw for refreshment during sleep, and at death for a longer period to take stock of our experience. In numerology the moon is given the number two, indicating the duality of the soul-life and the forces both of light and darkness which continually play upon it.

White Eagle says, 'As the still water reflects the sky, so the calm soul reflects the image of Christ.'* That lunar or hidden side of our nature is called negative because it absorbs and reflects impressions from the outside world, from the people in our environment, from their thoughts and actions as well as to register comfort and discomfort, pleasant and painful sensations. Our reaction to all these stimuli, combined with our inner awareness of the purpose of this present incarnation produces the personality our family and friends know. They recognise our physical and visible side through their five positive senses, but that part of us which is hidden, the soul-side, they sense through their own invisible or 'dark' self.

This lunar self is responsive both to the pull of the earth through the coarser elements of being, and to the attraction of the great light, the spiritual sun, the Creator. It is formed of the impressions not only of the small personality of this life but of the many personalities of many lives.

As we enter the Aquarian Age man is on the verge of learning secrets about the creative power deep within his being which will transform life on earth. The stuff from which our physical bodies are both created and destroyed is absolutely subject to the power of thought—either to

* Grace Cooke, *Meditation* (White Eagle Publishing Trust, 1965), p. 99. This book is an ideal sequel to the present one.

good thought, God-thought, put forth from the Christ-centre within the heart; or to the destructive thought from the undisciplined elemental side of our being, the unploughed field. These latter, coarser elements to which we so readily respond are yet the fertile ground of life and nourishment from which our own beautiful tree of life is created, when through the projection of God-thought and through the constant effort of the Christ-self the whole being is raised into unity with God.

By our habitual thought we shape our bodies. Our habits of mind show in our facial expression, voice, gestures and gait, and in the parts of our body which later in life show wear and tear because of strain and tension. Sometimes strong souls who have glimpsed the glory of God are fired with a great desire to work quickly through their karmic debts and therefore return to the physical life with more than the usual share of physical disability. Experience of pain or humiliation stirs within the creative waters of the soul a pure current of love and compassion. It will free them from the karma of past ignorance and self-will and greatly increase their power for service and joy in the future. The same may be said of the extreme emotional suffering which some souls have to bear. Suffering forces them to find the light within their soul, and they are able to draw strength from it. When the outer life runs smoothly and pleasurably there is less in-

centive to search for the living water within. It is usually only in sorrow or sickness that the need for God is felt.

Although we can do little to alter the karma resulting from past thought and action, the future is wholly ours. Minute by minute, hour by hour, our present thought is creating the body, the outlook and the conditions of the future. Few of us realise the urgency, even from a purely selfish point of view, of gaining control of our thought. The thoughts and spontaneous reactions of the lower parts of that invisible lunar self pour as an unending stream incessantly through the mind, our automatic response to the changing astrological conditions within ourselves and in the world outside. It is quite an interesting exercise to stand aside from our everyday thoughts and as a dispassionate observer recognise the host of different ideas, impressions, odd thoughts and reactions passing through us. Even with work which fully exercises our concentration, extraneous thoughts and ideas often enter unbidden. It is a disciplined soul indeed who has absolute control of his own mind, because his being is united with the Solar Logos, from which all light, all health, and all wisdom flow.

Perhaps the most vital aspect of White Eagle's teaching is to help men to gain such control over their thoughts that they are constantly creating and radiating light, peace, harmony in themselves and their surroundings. Concentrated thought gives power and life to the object of concentration. If our thoughts are constantly focused upon earthly things, limited by fear of losing earthly possessions or physical and emotional well-being, we gradually build into our souls a heavy cloud of anxiety and suspicion which eventually manifests in a sick body. If, on the other hand, our thoughts are by constant effort and discipline focused upon God; if we constantly remind ourselves of the beautiful creative power of the lord of life or even upon the spiritual teacher to whom we look for guidance, we are building into the soul a peace and beauty which will manifest in a body full of light even when that body is still showing the effects of past karma.

To help us in this work of wisely focusing our thought power White Eagle has given us from the brotherhood of light a symbol, the shining six-pointed star. This is the symbol of man made perfect, perfectly polarised between heaven and earth. The upward-pointing equilateral triangle indicates the outer self firmly based on earth, but with thought and feeling reaching heavenwards, aspiring towards heavenly guidance and communion. The downward-pointing triangle represents the inner self, shining into man from the heavenly state. This perfect blending of the invisible or inner self with the earthly personality and body is the crown of our endeavour. The shining star, the Pole Star of our being, represents not only the Christing of each individual but the great Christ Star in the heavens, and thus is interpreted as God personified, the Son of God.

The shining six-pointed star is a most compelling focal point for thought. If we want to control the multitudinous thought-images which throng the brain, we need a powerful magnet which will gradually compel our full attention. The finest way to combat negative thoughts and fears is to turn our attention from them to this radiant star. Followers of the White Eagle teaching are encouraged to think of the star every three hours, at 3.00, 6.00, 9.00 and 12.00, in order not only to bring about thought-control, but also to radiate the divine light into the soul-world to bring healing and peace to humanity.

The thought of the star can be wonderfully helpful at times when we are shocked or upset, deeply hurt or full of fear for ourselves or for loved ones. The immediate reaction of the little earthly personality is to mill over the incident. The sad thoughts, the fear, the anger, go round and round in the brain until we are distraught and may react to others in a sharp, angry way, thus only extending the area of disturbance. But if immediately the shock hits us we turn our thoughts to that still radiant star and concentrate on its strength and peace and beauty, we soon begin to feel enveloped in a protective cloak of light. The light of the star becomes ever more clearly reflected in the still water of the soul and our own peace radiates to our

companions until the disturbance fades away. In times of deep emotional stress the battle with the disturbing forces will keep recurring and we need to do this constantly. To learn this may be one of the deeper purposes of the whole experience.

Few people realise how the power of the Christ star can be used to recreate and heal the physical body. The cells of the physical body are all in the control of the invisible self, which in essence is united with the divine Mother being. The cells of the physical body are destroyed constantly and renewed, the quality of that re-

13

newal being dependent upon the quality of our thought life. If we allow ourselves just to be carried along by the ordinary stream of thought which flows around us all the time, given average good fortune, the body will follow the natural cycle of youth, maturity, age and decay which is common to all physical form. Yet within each of us is a fountain of living water, a fountain of divine life which through aspiration can be allowed to rise up and re-vitalise every cell of the body. The White Eagle healing service includes the words 'Every cell of your body is subject to the divine power and glory. Hold fast to the certainty that Christ within you is king and can overcome all weakness, all sickness, all inharmony'.

With physical sickness, as with mental and emotional disturbance, the first thing we have to do is to try to withdraw our thought from the nagging ache or pain or the fear. Inevitably this is a hard task, because the physical body is the final testing-ground of the spirit, but concentration on the shining star will always help to draw the mind away from the physical disease. Even with severe pain, if the mind is fixed upon the star, it is possible almost unconsciously to become detached from the physical body and to become, as it were, an observer.

The ability to focus the consciousness on the star grows with practice. It is not a fierce battle but a gentle persistence, a constant effort to withdraw one's attention to the Source. It is a good idea to practise this every night before sleeping, for even in health the physical atoms will gradually respond and produce increasingly fresh, vital tissue.

So last thing every night relax into the most comfortable sleep-position, and consciously release tension in every joint and muscle, especially at the back of the neck, and in the tongue and the jaw. The yoga practice of methodically tensing and relaxing every part of the body

from feet to head is helpful here. It really is worthwhile
practising this until it becomes habitual. Then quietly
practise breathing in the breath of God, three or four
times, relaxing even more. Be quietly aware of the even
rhythm of your breathing.

Now gently and peacefully feel that you are in the ray
of the beautiful shining star, so still, so radiant. You are
breathing in the light from that still white star in the
heart of the Sun. Your whole being is filled with light.
The star, your real Christ-self, is shining in your heart,
growing brighter with each gentle, peaceful breath. Now
quietly speak the words, 'Divine light shines in me.
Divine life permeates and heals every atom of my being. I
AM the resurrection and the life.' Repeat these words
slowly and distinctly three times with your whole being
focused on the star.

Now if there is some specific part of the body that
needs special recreation repeat the mantram again, drawing the light to that particular part as follows: 'Divine
Light shines in me. Divine life permeates and heals my
(knees, back, eyes, ears, digestion, heart, etc.). I AM the
resurrection and the life.' Repeat this three times very
gently and peacefully, and then say again the first affirmation; and finally just relax the whole being knowing
deep within that you are in this beautiful Christ ray.

In this method of attuning yourself to your own creative source don't try to do too much at a time. Only pay
attention to one part of the body, seeing it permeated
with the renewing Christ-life, then go back to the complete absorption in the light. The less you think about
specific troubles, the better. The whole object is to detach
your consciousness from bodily ills and focus it in the
Christ-self, that part of you which is divine and which
must eventually bring the perfection of divine life through
into physical manifestation. Do it without fail, actually

speaking the words (or mouthing them if you share a room or a bed). The action of the organs of speech—even if you only whisper—helps to crystallise the thought.

This gentle, regular effort of attuning yourself with the Christ-life is especially valuable if you are receiving spiritual healing. It is also helpful if you long to give healing. Night and morning are the best times for this practice, when the outer mind is either quietened down before sleeping, or not yet fully back in action. Only when the positive everyday mentality is in abeyance does the divine will within you take command, and shine on the still waters of your soul, permeating that deeper self with God-thought which will gradually manifest in improved physical health and well-being.

# 3
## *The Four Elements*

The astrological glyph for the earth is the equal-sided cross within the circle, an ancient symbol which is found all over the world. The cross signifies the imprisonment of the soul in matter, its coming into a body of flesh and into circumstances created by its own past actions and reactions. The circle is the universal love of God which enfolds it in incarnation. It also signifies the great circle of the heavens, the apparent path of the Sun and planets through the sky, which we know as the zodiac. Thus all that lives is encompassed by the Sun, which from the earliest times has symbolised not only the love of God, but also the heart of man and the love which radiates from it. Nothing that happens, on earth or in the heavens, is outside that divine love. Love is the law of all life—a law which is beautifully expounded in the ancient science of astrology.

'The esoteric astrologer,' says Alan Leo, 'looks upon the whole expression of life as proceeding from one central and primal source, and therefore seeks to understand the subject from the point of view of the One flowing forth into the many. . . .

'Man, as we know him, is composed of the great elements Fire, Air, Water, Earth and Ether. At the head of each of these is a living, conscious entity of which the vital force and consciousness flowing through the element is an emanation. . . .

'The one and supreme Cause of all is the God of very God, the unnameable Being and substance from which all the mighty Intelligences of the whole universe have come forth. Living and moving in the vast ocean of Being and Substance of which the Absolute is both centre and circumference, are millions of universes and solar systems. These are units having a Sun or Logos at the centre; the Sun being the physical and outward glory of the Spiritual Intelligence or supreme consciousness whose whole Being is the solar system with its planets and mighty centres of consciousness seen and unseen by physical sight.'*

In the cross within the circle, the symbol of the planet Earth, the arms represent the four elements, fire, earth, air and water, which constitute and govern our life in the physical body, and bring to the soul its major experiences or initiations. We all have the four elements manifesting to a greater or lesser degree in our physical constitution, our mind and our character, as well as in the circumstances of our outer life.

The fire element is closely related to the sun and teaches the soul the lessons of love in all its many aspects. It is the element of inspiration, vision, enthusiasm, warmth, vitality and energy. It engenders faith and confidence in the God above and the God within, and when strong in a person's make-up it gives them enthusiasm, hope and a strong tendency to impulsive action. It is perhaps the most heroic and the most foolhardy of the elements. Until some wisdom and discrimination have been gained, the rebellious desire nature can lead the soul into many difficulties and conflicts, resulting in pain and sorrow, which exert a cleansing, purging effect. In the body the fire element is concerned with the heart and the circulation, also the head.

The earth element is concerned with the practical issues of everyday life, money, possessions, employment,

---

* *Esoteric Astrology* (L. N. Fowler, 1925), p. xiv.

physical health, career. It teaches the soul the lesson of service. This is the element of rigid commonsense and realism, which doubt the validity of anything not immediately perceptible to the five senses. Predominantly earthy people are practical, capable and reliable, but not given to flights of imagination. They cannot entirely understand the inspiration and idealism of the more fiery

and airy types, yet without such stimulation they tend towards depression, worry and lethargy. In the body this element is concerned with the bony framework, the flesh and the skin.

Air is the element of the mind. It stimulates the desire for companionship, for communication and the exchange of ideas, and it brings to the soul the lessons of brotherhood. People with this element predominant have highly sensitive nervous systems and keen minds which are open to inspiration from the higher worlds. They can readily understand and interpret abstract ideas, and are often full of theories which do not necessarily work out in practice. While they are friendly and companionable, they also have a certain detachment from their companions and shy away from too much emotional involvement. This element is chiefly concerned with the nervous system, breathing and speech, also the circulation of the life-force round the body.

Water is the element of sympathetic emotion, and people with this element emphasised in their constitution are often the caring ones of the community. They need emotional involvement. They feel with others and instinctively understand their needs. They love to care for others, children, animals, sick people, plants—all living things. They tend to live much in the feeling side of their nature and psychically they absorb the conflicts and cares of others. They can easily become disturbed and emotionally overwrought, either with depression or elation, and need to learn how to still the emotions, so that the waters of the soul mirror the calm beauty of the heavens rather than the conflicts of the earth. The soul lesson of the water element is divine peace.

Everyone has to learn how to balance this cross of the elements within their own life and being. So often in life the arms of the cross pull in different directions. We stretch ourselves upon it as we reach out to grasp material success, physical ease and comfort, or emotional satisfaction which we think will bring us happiness and fulfilment. 'I want, I want, I want,' 'Give me, give me, give me,' we cry. Our eager hands stretch out to grasp and to hold more and more, to satisfy selfish desires and ambitions, so that we are pulled first one way and then the other by the conflict which we set in motion in ourselves and in our environment. In time the tension—the disappointments and frustrations and even the elations and excitements—becomes too much for the nervous system, so that sickness results.

The cross also demonstrates for us the law of balance which ensures that every thought and action brings its appropriate reaction in mind and body. We reap as we sow throughout eternity, and the chronic disease of this life usually springs from seeds of conflict and selfishness sown in the past. No matter how successfully we reach out and grasp according to our human desires, the time must come when the lord of life says, 'No, my child. No, you cannot have that—by your thought and actions you have forfeited the right.'

When everything is easy and peaceful there is no incentive to turn within. It is only when life grows difficult, when we suffer frustration or world weariness that we begin to cry out, 'Oh God, help me.' The inner flame lies dormant. Instead of reaching out to grasp at satisfaction for mind and senses we begin to seek the still place at the centre of the cross—the sanctuary deep within. 'O God, give me strength.' As we pray to God with our whole being, we feel a strength arising from we know not where. We take an hour, a day, at a time, doing our best in humility and prayer, and we begin to realise that a peaceful acceptance is growing—a confidence in this hidden source of strength.

Like a little flame in the heart, our prayer rises in silent aspiration, and from the great circle of the heavens, the circle of universal love, the light pours down, bringing comfort, illumination and protection. The flame within blends with the light from above, and the star of Christ-love is born in the heart. That star brings sure conviction that we are children of God, that God's light shines upon our path. We begin to realise that no matter what tests and conflicts of the elements may come, what hard cross of matter has to be faced, the circle of God's love enfolds us. We are utterly safe and at peace.

As we learn consciously to attune ourselves to the Pole Star of our innermost being, we are linked with the centre of the cosmos—all wisdom, love and power. From this source there flows through us a radiation of light and love to the Christ in every being. All are one—there is no separation, no death; we are in eternity. This Christ Star in the heart draws all men into brotherhood. Such a brotherhood comprises not only life in physical form, but life in the etheric and soul-world which will be revealed to the soul as it learns to find the Pole Star of its own being.

As the higher mind, the mind in the heart, becomes awakened, we begin to discover the reality of the angelic kingdoms and to have inner feelings of the planetary angels, of the angels of the elements, and of the teeming life in the etheric world or the 'fairy kingdom' of nature. In ESOTERIC ASTROLOGY, Alan Leo writes of this angelic host: 'If we could look into the angelic world we should be amazed at the wonderful evolution that is going on there in a realm that is as real and as important as the other divisions of nature of which we are more fully conscious, namely the mineral, vegetable, animal and human kingdoms. Each angel has his place in that world as humans have in this, but they are moved by one will, that of the supreme Intelligence who is both the heart and brain of all; and although they have far greater power than any human being, they are limited and restricted to their own particular sphere of operations. Many names have been applied to these angels, but the Hindu astrologers have always termed them Devas, which means Shining or Radiant, owing to their bodies being formed of the bright luminous matter of the plane to which they belong.'

Earlier Alan Leo says, 'These are specially connected with the manifold subdivisions of the seven great rays that are constantly streaming through the seven planetary spheres of influence. The fact that there is a great evolution beyond the human in which there are grades of those beings called angels, from the mighty archangels down to the minor elementals should surprise no one who has even a faint knowledge of religion, since all religions teach that the work of creation began with the calling into existence of a vast host of intelligent Beings of varying power and authority, into whose care was entrusted the special work of guiding and controlling the activities of nature.'*

Awareness of the presence of angels is not a gift limited to a chosen few although, probably through training in past lives, some people may be more spontaneously perceptive than others. The angelic world mingles closely with our human state. Artists, musicians and poets through the ages have sensed this, and some have acknowledged angelic inspiration; but the most down-to-earth people can with a little effort and dedication train themselves to become more aware of angelic help in their lives. Every human soul has a guardian angel who is its constant companion. This beautiful being comes to guide the life of the child of earth along its own planetary ray. In the really big issues of life the soul has little choice. Something drives it to take certain action. Sometimes there comes a time of testing when the angel points out two paths, either of which can be followed, and the soul has to make the choice, usually between following the whisper of conscience or the dictates of self-will and personal desire. The decision having been made, the path has to be followed and the guardian angel watches every step of the way, leading the soul through the experiences of earth to learn the deep lessons of its own planetary ray.

In order consciously to contact the angelic world and the beings of the etheric kingdom, one vital quality has to

* *Esoteric Astrology*, pp. 122, 123.

be cultivated. This is inner stillness. It is a conscious let-ting-go of all the excitements, the tensions, the desires, the interests of the outer mind. Many people are so anxious to see into the inner world, so eager for psychic experi-ence, that they palpitate with excitement, enthusiasm and maybe apprehension also. This state of mind closes the door firmly on the possibility of conscious contact. The outer mind is just too eager and too brash to be able to touch or comprehend this inner world, even though it is so close to the physical.

One does not see angels with physical sight and fierce concentration of the outer mind. Awareness of their pre-sence steals upon us as with quiet breathing and con-scious relaxation we make the mind like a still lake re-flecting the sky and the surrounding countryside. 'As the still water reflects the sky, so the calm soul reflects the image of Christ.'

In this state of peaceful stillness and surrender the sun of the inner consciousness, the true solar self, begins to rise and illumine the whole scene. The still water reflects the glory of that light. Slight movement on the surface of the water will break up that pure white light into many sparkling rainbow colours. As we become ever more still, surrendering our whole being to the sun, the beautiful colours gradually take form as pillars of light which we may perceive as winged beings of indescribable beauty and stillness. One of these winged beings has charge over your soul. In the stillness of your heart-consciousness, for this is what you are now touching, you will become aware of the sun as your greater self, the power behind your life which will give you sure direction and clear vision con-cerning your future path and your present action. As in utter surrender you quietly focus your attention on this inner sun, the angel who is your guardian in this life enfolds you in beautiful wings of light, the colour of your own particular planetary ray, and in your heart you will hear the voice of his direction. Angels are usually perfectly-balanced dual beings who show both the masculine or feminine, positive or receptive qualities as needed.

When in difficulties or beset by problems many people dissipate physical and psychic energy, in rushing hither and thither seeking advice and counsel. Of course, on the physical plane, when dealing with material problems it is sensible where possible to seek trained, expert advice. But in soul-problems, in problems of human relationships and the trials and sorrow of the inner life, there is only one sure source of help. This comes through the guardian angel and the guide to the soul who trains himself to become absolutely still in mind and spirit and attuned to the sun rising within the heart, the sun which is the true self.

As we learn to meditate in this way the inner world becomes more and more real. At first the spiritual life, the guides, the nature spirits, the angels, may seem to be part of a misty world which we only hope is real and true. But with steadfast persistence in meditation, the etheric world becomes more real and almost unconsciously we develop the awareness of angelic help in our physical life. We begin to function on an extra level, using the outer mind, the physical brain, for purely practical affairs, but bringing into operation also another much deeper consciousness, which brings such refreshment to the outer mind that it becomes more capable and efficient, more able to discriminate between the important and the unimportant, the real and the unreal.

When walking in the country, beside the sea, or working in the garden, if rather than thinking with the active outer mind, 'Oh I wish I could see the fairies', we became still and peacefully concentrated on the spiritual sun, or the star within, almost unnoticed an awareness of the etheric world, the etheric counterpart of all created things could steal upon us. Angels come upon you unawares. Try to chase them and catch them with the outer mind and they dissolve into nothingness. It is all a question of learning to bring into operation this deeper consciousness. Watch the birds; watch little animals; watch all growing things in nature. To watch them properly you need to become so still that you almost disappear into the landscape. You will notice that the wild creatures all know how to be still. A good deal of their time is spent silently sensing, becoming aware of their surroundings.

There are times however when angelic intervention in human life can be decisive and definite. Many people can relate stories of how by just missing a train they were spared a fatal accident, or how a sudden change of plan caused them to meet someone who deeply affected the

26

whole course of their life. As a child I experienced such an angelic intervention, which probably saved my life and certainly prevented a severe accident. We were living in the country and our cooking was done on an oil stove. One day I went to fill the stove with a can which should have contained paraffin and very clearly I heard the words, 'Stop! that is petrol'. As far as I knew there was no earthly reason why petrol should be in the can, which always stood near the cooker, ready to replenish the tank, but the voice was so commanding that I stopped. I smelt the contents and felt a little unsure so I took the can to my parents. My father experimented by putting a drop or two on a fire which had been laid and putting a match to it. The resulting mild explosion convinced us both that my angel had certainly been on guard! I shall never forget the command in the voice which said, 'Stop!'.

No doubt many people can point to instances such as this in which their lives, or health, have been saved by some inexplicable intervention. It is the work of the guardian angel of every soul to see that it is protected from experiences which are not in the plan of its destiny and guided to be in the right place at the right time to undergo a necessary experience.

Students of occultism know that there are many different types and degrees of angels. No matter what form of service we have been drawn to in this day of life, we can perform it more efficiently, more happily as we learn to call upon the help of the fairies and angels of the particular element in which we are working. There is much to be learnt about these angelic helpers which cannot be found in any book. The inner knowledge can only be revealed gradually to the soul through the life-experience, and as he or she responds more completely to the love of God in the heart and it shines through the life in loving service to all creation.

27

It seems a pity that the habit of daily prayer and aspiration has fallen out of fashion. Prayers which are gabbled off so quickly and automatically that they mean nothing are of little use, but the habit of true prayer, prayer which is really meditation, contemplation and worship of the eternal spirit, is the gateway to the heavenly places and a sure method of invoking the help of the angels.

# 4

## *The Seven-Ray System in Nature*

The Lords of the seven rays which pour forth from the spiritual Sun are sometimes known as the sons of the flame, or as the angels round the throne of God. From these seven rays all creation comes into being. All mineral, plant, animal or human life is permeated by these planetary forces. In the mineral kingdom this penetration is a latent force awaiting development, but it gives the metal, stone or jewel its own special vibration. In plant life the quickening ray of the planet manifests in more complex form. In the animal kingdom there comes a blending of planetary influences; while at the human stage the soul represents a universe in miniature, which the ray of the sun links directly with the Solar Logos. All the planetary rays playing upon that soul intermingle to produce the myriad variations in physical, mental and psychic characteristics. The spirit of man, the Christ within, has so to rule his own universe that all the elements harmoniously combine to produce the perfect Sun-man or Sun-woman.

The whole solar universe is so marvellously governed, the planetary angels so perfectly organised, each in his own sphere, that the tiniest detail of life is within the divine, immutable law.

Minerals, plants and animals all evolve under the care of planetary angels, who range from the great beings round the throne right down to the tiny nature spirits who actually work with the earth, the precious stones and with plant life. Animals too evolve under the direction of

29

their own group spirits. When, however, we regard the human level, new conditions operate. In the bible we are told that God made man in His own image, fashioning him out of the dust (all the elements, which under the direction of planetary intelligences constitute form) and then breathing into him the divine breath, the eternal life of the sun. In other words God gives to man the seed of light, the power to develop an individual God-consciousness which will ultimately gain control of the planetary system of his own being and throughout nature. Deep within man lies the seed from which will grow the tree of life.

Man has also the gift of freewill and knowledge of good and evil: he knows both the heavenly pull and the pull of the earth, and must find the point of perfect balance between the two. At a stage during his descent into matter the pull of the earth becomes all-powerful, as he seeks knowledge and earth-experience. As the soul uses the gift of freewill, the law of cause and effect comes into operation, as well as the other great laws governing human life (the laws of equilibrium and opportunity), which bring him the wisdom he needs.

The God-men, beings from the sphere of the sun who come to help each cycle of incoming souls on their evolutionary path, brought to humanity knowledge of the healing power of herbs, mineral substances, and even jewels according to their planetary rays. From ancient times wise men have studied the effect of plants and herbs on the human body and soul, and once it was customary for physicians to treat patients according to their horoscopes. Physicians knew of the subtle connection between the planets and all growing things, and would select herbs which, because of the influence of the ruling planet, would help to bring about a more harmonious balance of the elements. For instance, if the patient's horoscope showed an overbalance of the fiery element, through dominance of the planet Mars, the physician might prescribe herbs coming under Saturn and Venus, to cool the bloodstream and bring about a gentler and less aggressive state of mind. On the other hand, if a naturally fiery patient had exhausted himself with overstrain, then herbs coming under Mars would be given to restore vitality. Nicholas Culpeper's herbal (1653) gives detailed instructions for prescribing herbs either in sympathy or antipathy with the patient's planetary rulers.

Diagnosis and prescription of herbs by astrology requires more knowledge and experience than is possessed by most practitioners today, and in many cases the astrologer meets a well-nigh insuperable obstacle in the patient's ignorance of his time of birth. A modern doctor with a large general practice would hardly have time to set up horoscopes for all his patients, even given the necessary data! Nevertheless, as the Aquarian Age advances the time must surely come when spiritual and physical science will draw closer to each other. Students will understand more fully what is in fact the law of correspondences, namely that all forms of life on the earth, and even the rocks and minerals, are in sympathetic harmony with the stars and planets. They will know that deeply-rooted disease comes because of broken rhythm, or a lack of balance and harmony in man's subtler bodies. Certain herbs, colours, and even rocks and stones affect these subtler bodies, helping to release tensions and congestion, and to restore the free flow of the life-forces in the aura. This restoration of harmony will soon bring about a cleansing and healing of the physical symptoms.

In mediaeval times it was usual for those who could afford to do so to wear a ring or some kind of jewelled ornament linked with their own planet or zodiacal sign. With the ever-increasing public interest in astrology this

31

is again becoming fashionable, especially among young people. Sensitives find that wearing their own birth-stone or metal helps to quicken their response to the angels of that particular ray. Unfortunately there is a certain amount of disagreement among the authorities as to these planetary relationships, especially the relationships between colours and sounds.

There is a further significance of the seven-ray system, closely related to the four elements and the twelve signs of the zodiac. In a spirit message, reprinted in THE RETURN OF ARTHUR CONAN DOYLE, Sir Arthur says, 'We declare that all human life is divided into rays of varying vibrations and that it is ruled by such rays. . . . In this connection we would direct your minds to the twelve "signs" of the zodiac, to the twelve "tribes" of Israel, to the mystery and significance of the number "twelve" . . . . Every herb comes under one or other of these twelve rays.'*

If however these rays are based on the twelve signs of the zodiac, why then do we refer so much to seven planetary rays? There is a close correspondence between the twelve and the seven for the seven planetary rulers affect life on earth, through the twelve signs of the zodiac. This we shall see in relation to the subdivisions of the year.†

Our seven-day week is linked with the time taken by the moon to travel round the earth, just as the months of the year are linked with the passage of the sun through the signs of the zodiac.

The days of the week are named after the planets, including the Sun and Moon, which rule each one of them as it dawns. There are however three systems of classifica-

* Ed. Ivan Cooke (White Eagle Publishing Trust, 1980) pp. 161–7.
† Those interested in numerology will also recognise a link in the fact that the number seven is three plus four, and the number twelve is three times four. The intimate and intrinsic relationship between the numbers 3 and 4 is demonstrated in the tetrahedron, or the solid equilateral triangle, which has four faces, each with three sides.

tion. From ancient times, before the discovery of the ones beyond Saturn, the planets have been listed in order of their rapidity of motion, starting either with Saturn, the slowest, or the Moon, the fastest. The best-known classification of the days is according to the planetary hours, starting from Friday midnight to 1 a.m. on Saturday, this first hour being under the rulership of Saturn, and giving its name to the day. The next hour comes under Jupiter, the next under Mars, and so on in the following order: Saturn, Jupiter, Mars, Sun, Venus, Mercury, Moon. This follows through the whole twenty-four hours, which makes the planetary ruler of the first hour of the next day the Sun, giving its name to Sunday, and so on right through the week.

The French names for some of the days more clearly indicate the planetary ruler than the English ones. For instance, 'Mardi' shows Tuesday to be Mars' day, similarly 'Mercredi' shows Wednesday to be Mercury's, and 'Vendredi' shows Friday to be the day of Venus. Some of the English names are linked with the Norse gods, but they are all associated with the same planetary principles.

Alan Leo, in ESOTERIC ASTROLOGY, gives two different classifications, both founded on occult fact.* Of these, one results from the day being divided into four quarters, the first beginning shortly before sunrise on Monday, which is so called because its first quarter is ruled by the Moon,

|   | Monday | Tuesday | Wednesday | Thursday | Friday | Saturday | Sunday |
|---|--------|---------|-----------|----------|--------|----------|--------|
| 1 | *Moon* | *Mars* | *Mercury* | *Jupiter* | *Venus* | *Saturn* | *Sun* |
| 2 | *Mercury* | *Jupiter* | *Venus* | *Saturn* | *Sun* | *Moon* | *Mars* |
| 3 | *Venus* | *Saturn* | *Sun* | *Moon* | *Mars* | *Mercury* | *Jupiter* |
| 4 | *Sun* | *Moon* | *Mars* | *Mercury* | *Jupiter* | *Venus* | *Saturn* |

* p. 252

33

which thus exercises a general rulership over the whole day. Its second quarter, starting at noon, comes under Mercury; its third, at the moment of sunset, by Venus; and its fourth, at midnight, by the Sun. If the planets are listed vertically from fastest to slowest, the table above results.

This fourfold division compares with the four elements in the zodiac as symbolised by the cross within the circle.

Just the same result, as far as the days are concerned, comes from a threefold division, linked with the three qualities of the zodiac, the signs being described as cardinal, fixed or mutable. Apparently this division of the day into three equal parts was used in ancient Egypt. In this classification, we begin the order of planets with the slowest, Saturn, resulting in the following table.

|   | Saturday | Sunday | Monday | Tuesday | Wednesday | Thursday | Friday |
|---|----------|--------|--------|---------|-----------|----------|--------|
| 1 | *Saturn* | *Sun* | *Moon* | *Mars* | *Mercury* | *Jupiter* | *Venus* |
| 2 | *Jupiter* | *Venus* | *Saturn* | *Sun* | *Moon* | *Mars* | *Mercury* |
| 3 | *Mars* | *Mercury* | *Jupiter* | *Venus* | *Saturn* | *Sun* | *Moon* |

So whichever method we use, the planetary rulers remain constant, and give to each day its own planetary angels whose energies can be absorbed in meditation and used to bring greater harmony to everyday life.

Our knowledge of the planetary rulership of plants, jewels, colours and musical tones is fragmentary and incomplete today, and obviously a great deal of research will have to be undertaken before the ancient wisdom can be brought back into full use. Spiritual and physical scientists will need to co-operate in order to test the individual radiation of plants and gems, and the vibratory rates of colours and tones, so as to link them to their appropriate planetary rays. Perhaps one day, too, birth certificates will be issued in the form of computer-produced natal horoscopes—so that medical treatment, computerised in accordance with the soul's 'ray', can easily be prescribed.

A certain amount of research has taken place linking the biochemic salts to the signs of the zodiac, and prescribing according to the horoscope of the patient, but again our knowledge is tantalisingly incomplete, and very few astrologers specialise in the medical branch of this subject.

The late Dr Edward Bach devoted his life to discovering 'the twelve healers'—herbs that would treat emotional and mental states rather than physical symptoms. As far as we know, he was not concerned with astrology, but his close observation of human nature in sickness and health during his busy years of orthodox medical practice led him to the conclusion that all physical symptoms had their roots in soul-inharmonies. So convinced did he become that he withdrew from orthodox medicine and devoted the rest of his life to discovering the special herbs with power to heal inharmonious mental and emotional states. In many cases the herb he prescribes for a certain mental state comes under the rulership of a planet which an astrologer would recognise as being particularly helpful in its influence on that condition. For instance, Dr Bach recommended the flower gentian for those easily discouraged by small delays and hindrances. Gentian comes under the ray of Mars, planet of fire, energy, courage and endurance, qualities which are obviously needed by one easily discouraged. Another martian herb, gorse, he prescribes for those who feel ready to succumb in hopeless resignation to their difficulties. Here again the fighting qualities of Mars need to be strengthened in the soul.

The planet Jupiter is specially associated with the

higher mind, and brings qualities of hopefulness, aspiration and spiritual peace. Dr Bach recommends red chestnut for those who are over-anxious about the welfare of others, and white chestnut for those suffering inability to control sorrowful and disquieting thoughts. Both of these are ruled by Jupiter.

Undoubtedly a wealth of knowledge regarding the planetary rays and the forces in the etheric world which can be harnessed for the benefit of man awaits our discovery, or rediscovery, during the Aquarian Age; we are only on the fringe of understanding these subtler energies which can be released as man himself awakens to the tremendous inner life of the soul-world. This is why meditation is of such importance, for through it the consciousness expands to include that higher dimension in which deeper understanding and reverence for life at all levels of being is felt.

In the following table of planetary rulerships, the colours are according to Alan Leo, the herbs and plants according to Nicholas Culpeper, and the jewels according to the occultist Manly Hall.

## The Sun
### Rules Leo, a fixed fire sign

COLOUR: orange or gold
PLANTS AND TREES include: angelica, ash, bay, camomile, campion, greater celandine, centaury, eyebright, juniper, marigold, mistletoe, pimpernel, rosemary, rue, saffron, sundew, St John's wort, tormentil, heart trefoil, heliotrope, walnut
METAL: gold
GEMS: ruby, hyacinth, carbuncle (the last two also under Jupiter), cat's-eye, and sometimes diamond

## The Moon

*Rules Cancer, a cardinal water sign*

COLOUR: Violet or amethyst

PLANTS AND TREES include: acanthus, adder's tongue, cabbage, chickweed, clary, cleavers (goose-grass), cucumber, lady's smock, loose-strife, orpine, poppy, privet, purselane, rattle-grass, saxifrage, stonecrop, pearl trefoil, wall-flower, watercress, waterlily, willow, white rose

METALS: silver, aluminium

GEMS: emerald, various crystals, pearls

## Mercury

*Rules Gemini, a mutable air sign, and*
*Virgo, a mutable earth sign*

COLOUR: pale yellow in Gemini; pale orange or corn colour in Virgo

PLANTS AND TREES include: caraway, carrots, dill, fennel (Virgo), fern, germander, hazelnut, honeysuckle, horehound, lavender, liquorice, lily-of-the-valley, maidenhair, marjoram, mulberry, parsley, cow-parsnip, scabious, southernwood, sow-fennel, valerian, woodbine

METAL: quicksilver

GEMS: agate, aquamarine, topaz, glass, marble

## Venus

*Rules Taurus, a fixed earth sign, and*
*Libra, a cardinal air sign*

COLOUR: gentle blue of forget-me-nots, tending towards

delphinium mauve, in Taurus; in Libra, gentle blues, tending towards the green and turquoise shades
PLANTS AND TREES include: alder, artichoke, beans, birch, blackberry, bugle, cherry, chickpea, columbine, cowslip, elder, endive, figwort, foxglove, golden rod, gooseberry, groundsel, herb robert, kidney wort, lady's bedstraw, lady's mantle, mallow, mint, meadowsweet, orchid, parsnip, pennyroyal, periwinkle, plantain, primrose, ragwort, damask rose, self-heal, sorrel, sow-thistle, strawberries, tansy, teazle, thistle, thyme, vervain, violets, wheat, yarrow
METALS: copper, brass
GEMS: cornelian, moss agate, coral, jade, alabaster, lapis lazuli, beryl, chrysolite


## Mars

### Rules Aries, a cardinal fire sign, and
### Scorpio, a fixed water sign

COLOURS: bright red-orange, scarlet or warm pink in Aries; rich deep crimson in Scorpio.
PLANTS AND TREES include: all-heal, anemone, barberry, basil (Scorpio), briony, broom, lesser celandine, chives, cresses, crowfoot, cuckoo-pint, cotton thistle, toad-flax, furze, garlic, gentian, hedge hyssop, hops, mustard, nettle, onion, pepperwort, radish, horseradish, rest-harrow, rocket rhubarb, thistle, tobacco (English), wormwood
METALS: iron, steel
GEMS: jasper, bloodstone, loadstone, flint, malachite, sometimes diamond

## Jupiter
*Rules Sagittarius, a mutable fire sign, and*
*Pisces, a mutable water sign*

COLOURS: indigo in Sagittarius; silvery blue-grey in Pisces
PLANTS AND TREES include: agrimony, asparagus, avens, balm, beets (also under Saturn), betony, bulberry, borage, bugloss, chervil, chestnut, cinque foil, dandelion, dock, gilliflower, clove, hart's tongue, houseleek, hyssop, liverwort, lungwort, maple, oak, red roses, sage, samphire, lady's thistle
METAL: tin
GEMS: amethyst, hyacinth (also under Sun), topaz, moonstone, carbuncle (also under Sun)


## Saturn
*Rules Capricorn, a cardinal earth sign, and*
*Aquarius, a fixed air sign*

COLOUR: dark rich green in Capricorn; lighter spring green in Aquarius
PLANTS AND TREES include: amaranthus, barley, beech, comfrey, cornflower, crosswort, darnel, dodder, water fern, flea-wort, fumitory, hawkweed, hawthorn, heartsease, black hellebore, hemlock, hemp, henbane, horsetail, holly, ivy, knapweed, moss, mullein, nightshade, poplar, quince, rushes, shepherd's purse, Solomon's seal, tamarisk, wintergreen, woad
METAL: lead
GEMS: sapphire, lapis lazuli, jet and non-precious stones

*

The planets Uranus, Neptune and Pluto are not included in the septenary systems handed down from the ancients, but there is some evidence for linking Uranus with the Sun in rulership of metals and jewels, and Neptune with the Moon. Manly Hall suggests amber as being under Uranus and ivory under Neptune. These outermost planets would appear to affect the subtler bodies, and people strongly under their influence should respond readily to spiritual healing and colour treatment.

It is possible also that the influence of these planets manifests through some of the powerful modern drugs which have such a pronounced effect on the mental state of patients.

Although there is so much concern because of the widespread use of drugs today, it may well be that through this very fact humanity is being led to a deeper understanding of the close interrelation of soul and body. It is interesting that these matters were especially brought into prominence while Pluto, traditionally the planet of the underworld and ruler of all that is hidden in the sub-conscious (and superconscious?), was passing through Virgo, the sign of health and medicine, between 1956 and 1972. Uranus, often known as 'the lightning flash', the planet of spiritual awakening, was also passing through this sign, which is closely linked with the etheric world. Undoubtedly their combined influence helped to stir humanity out of its spiritual lethargy. In many parts of the world pioneer souls are now working under the direction and protection of the Brothers in spirit to help mankind to an understanding of the brotherhood of all life.

# 5

## Response

*Look how the floor of heaven*
*Is thick inlaid with patens of bright gold;*
*There's not the smallest orb which thou behold'st*
*But in his motion like an angel sings,*
*Still quiring to the young-eyed cherubins;*
*Such harmony is in immortal souls,*
*But whilst this muddy vesture of decay,*
*Doth grossly close it in, we cannot hear it.*
                    (Shakespeare, *The Merchant of Venice*)

Alan Leo tells us that people respond to the various fac-
tors in their birth chart differently according to their
stage of spiritual development.* The young soul will respond only to the sign on the ascendant, the 'rising sign',
and to the position of the planets in the houses of his
chart. The man who is awakening to the inner soul-life,
however, will respond more and more to the indication of
the planets' position in the zodiac. Consciously or unconsciously he will build into his soul the qualities they
represent. Although the circumstances of his outer life
will naturally accord with the house-position of the planets, these outer circumstances will have less and less
power to trouble him as he lives more in his own harmonious soul-world and adjusts himself to life as he finds it.

   The third stage comes when the soul has made con-
siderable progress in creating the various vehicles it

* *Esoteric Astrology*, p. 289.

needs, through its response to and its ability to manage the cross of the elements of its own being. It then responds increasingly to a particular planetary ray. It is beginning to specialise and to work consciously with the angels of that particular ray. All the elements of its being will be perfectly controlled, and the man will no longer be disturbed by anger, depression, fear, anxiety or emotional excitement. He will be steadfast, secure and absolutely one-pointed in his devotion to the Eternal Spirit, the source of his being. All his energies will be channelled into the service of God and all creation. He will be what

would be recognised in the East as a self-realised soul, a master.

These are three quite definite stages of growth and unfoldment, which cannot be hurried. It is useless to expect a child in the playgroup to cope with a problem of advanced physics, but this does not mean that he may not have the makings of a brilliant physicist in a few years' time.

Take musical appreciation. Practically everyone can respond to and enjoy the beat of dance music. Most people like to listen to a tuneful melody which arouses their feelings, happy or sad. Only those whose ears are trained to listen can appreciate harmony and hear the interweaving of different melodies in a sonata or a symphony. Because of their deeper understanding they feel the joy of the music on more levels of their being. The rhythm stimulates physical response. The combination of melody and simple harmony stimulates emotional response while the fuller, richer understanding of the music calls for the response not only of the ordinary mind but the higher mind. Truly great musicians are consciously or unconsciously attuned to the celestial world. Sometimes this response puts such a strain on the nervous system and the etheric body that an artist will seem, to the less sensitively attuned, to behave strangely. The actions of a master are not always comprehensible to those who have not developed the same understanding.

Artists have a particular work to do. The response of each to the subtleties of his own particular medium opens him to inspiration and creativity. Many artists find that they begin by working on an idea but that at a certain point some greater power pours into them. The same may be true of scientists who make important discoveries. Louis Pasteur recognised his need for periods of quiet meditation when something outside himself seemed to bring illumination, to throw light on the problem. This is the work of the angels influencing the higher consciousness.

This is not quite the same as the type of mediumship which is spontaneous psychic awareness (often connected with a highly sensitive solar plexus). Although it can be very helpful, particularly in giving comfort to the recently bereaved, it can also be unreliable, depending very much on prevailing psychic conditions. Direct contact with the higher world and angelic inspiration require quite different soul-training. Just as the musician needs to develop his ear to catch subtleties of sound and harmony, so each soul will eventually learn to respond to the higher worlds, the inner worlds of his being, whence he will draw the inspiration he needs on his life's journey. In other words, each soul can quicken his inner ear to the harmonies of the spirit, and sharpen his inner sight to the world of light all about him, interpenetrating the physical worlds. Through quiet breathing—breathing in the breath of God—and meditating upon the life of God manifesting in all form, he can become so attuned to the world of light that even the death of the body, the loss of his loved ones does not disturb his deep peace and happiness. He knows true communion of spirit and for him there is no separation.

This communion of spirit may seem a remote dream to those in the early stages of training in meditation, but just as the ear slowly begins to distinguish chords, so constant, gentle practice in meditation will gradually attune the soul to the celestial harmonies. The aspirant will begin to feel a deeper peace, and the earthly trials, the ups and downs of daily life, will affect him less and less. He will perhaps suddenly notice that a happening on the outer plane which some months previously would have made him angry or depressed has hardly affected him. He has just accepted the situation with a shrug and a laugh and left it to be put right in God's good time. He becomes less opinionated as he realises that there are different dimensions of life and subtler harmonies to be understood. He begins to submit what were once strong personal views to the gentler wisdom of the Creator. He begins to see truth as a great jewel with many sparkling facets each reflecting in its own way the light of the great central sun.

Prayer and meditation, if they are to play their part in attuning the soul to the celestial harmonies, should be a regular daily practice, gentle but persistent. But as we have just seen, each day of the week comes under its own planetary ray. According to Dr Szekely, members of the

Essene Brotherhood, to which both Jesus and John the Baptist are believed to have belonged, practised their meditations according to the angel of the particular day of the week. Moreover, they were expected to meditate, as the Moslems pray, at specific times of day. White Eagle too suggests projecting the light into the world at specific times. For the Essenes, the hours for meditation were dawn, noon and sunset; for followers of White Eagle the hours for sending out the light are 3, 6, 9 and 12, but in view of practical difficulties the meditations during the working day have to be just a quick attunement of the higher mind to the star, even while the practical mind is coping with everyday difficulties. Nevertheless for those who earnestly desire to become more aware of the world of light, quiet meditation morning and evening is essential.

For astrologers and all those who would like to become more attuned to the celestial harmony of the planets, we hope the following suggestions for day-meditations will prove helpful. To find the planetary rulership for the periods of meditation, we are following the fourfold division of the day (the cross within the circle) taking the planets in order from the fastest to the slowest. This makes Monday the first day of the week and Sunday the seventh. The meditations suggested are for early morning and either sunset or just before retiring for the night.

Many people, especially mothers, may find that they have to wait until the family are dispatched to their various activities before they have a moment to call their own. As previously stated, the best times for meditation are on first waking, when the soul is still to some extent aware of the inner worlds, and the earthly mind not yet too active, and just before retiring, when again the earthly mind can let go of the concerns of the outer world. The mind needs to do this to allow the soul to find freedom and refreshment during the hours of sleep. In the East, sunset is an important hour for prayer; and following the table on page 33, we have taken the planetary ruler of the fourth quarter to preside over the evening meditation.

To prepare for meditation sit poised and upright, but comfortably, relaxing the head, neck and shoulders particularly. Cross your ankles, right over left, and cup your left hand in the palm of your right. It will probably be helpful slowly to perform one or two exercises to loosen the muscles and release the tension at the back of the neck so that the life-forces can flow freely. Gently shrug the shoulders, bringing them first forwards, then back and down, first tensing all the muscles, then enjoying the sense of relaxation. Drop the head forward, then very slowly rotate the head to the left, feeling the pull of the muscles on the right side of the shoulders. Pause for a second or two, then slowly roll the head backward; pause—but not too long in this position—then to the right; pause; and again forward. Do this very slowly two or three times, then change and rotate the head the same number of times in the opposite direction. Then gently raise the head until it forms a straight line with the spine and is beautifully poised. Try to feel that a line of light is gently pulling the top of the head upwards so that the chin is pulled in a little and there is a feeling of freedom at the back of the neck. Now feel that the light is pouring into the top of the head and down the spine from a brilliant star which is a few feet above the head.

Breathe gently and peacefully, rather more slowly than usual. Start by breathing out from the lungs what seems like every scrap of air, and even then a little more, until you feel almost tense with the effort. Then relax. Let the air fill the lungs easily and peacefully; and realise that this air is charged with divine light, filling the bloodstream with new life and vitality; cleansing, healing, restoring every cell of the body. Hold the breath for a second or two; feel it recharging the bloodstream; then breathe out, consciously radiating light from the heart-centre in a joyous giving to all the world. Breathe out and out and out again, then once again become recharged with sunlight. If you are experienced in deep breathing you can do this seven times, but if you are only beginning do not take the full deep breath more than three times, or you may feel a little giddy. Return to the more normal breathing but at a slightly slower rhythm and focus your thought peacefully on the meditation for the day.

As you become more practised, you may well become so absorbed in your meditations that you find it difficult to return to the earthly consciousness; but earthly tasks must be fulfilled if we are to be instruments of the spirit. To help yourself come back into the earthly conscious-ness, again breathe deeply and 'think' yourself firmly back. Open your eyes and sit quietly for a few moments re-establishing control over the physical consciousness. You may find it helpful to seal your solar plexus centre by drawing over it with your right hand the symbol of the equal-sided cross within the circle. See it as a shield of silver light, then sit for a few seconds with your hands clasped in front of the solar plexus until you feel quite ready to take up the day's duties.

Until you become well practised in meditation it is wise to limit the time to about twenty minutes, which is prob-ably all you can spare; but as you grow accustomed to making the spiritual contact, it will become so precious to you that you will want to give yourself more time. Always, though, you must be aware of the need to pre-serve a good balance between the inner and outer life. The practice of meditation should make you more alert and capable in the performance of your earthly duties, not less.

47

# 6

## Meditations for the Days of the Week

MONDAY    *The day of the Moon*

*Morning meditation*

The angel of the Moon is essentially an angel of creative activity and power, but as we sit quietly breathing in the light let us remember that this day of the Moon is also associated with soul-magic, the inner or hidden side of life which lies behind all practical activity. Monday is for most people a particularly busy day, with much to be attended to after the weekend, but owing to the duality of the Moon's ray it also offers the possibility of touching a deep, subtle spiritual power. The Pole Star is astronomically linked with the constellation of Cancer, and as we attune ourselves to the angels of the Moon it is particularly helpful to imagine that we are under the rays of a shining six-pointed star, the sun of our innermost being, which shines out as a beautiful light in the darkness of matter as the triangles of the higher and lower self become perfectly blended. Continue breathing peacefully and slowly and feel the rays of the still, shining star quietening down the tension and stress of worldly concerns.

Now imagine a ripened seed, charged with life-force from the sun which has been carried down into the darkness of the soil. The nourishment of the earth combined with the rain from above calls into activity the life of the seed. We begin to understand the duality of the great mother of form, the soul of the world, when we see how the roots are drawn strongly downwards into the

48

dark earth to find nourishment for shoots which are drawn upwards into the light of the sun. This duality is essential to the Moon, and meditation on the growth of the seed will help us to understand how and why the soul of man is drawn into incarnation; how life in the physical body is like the planting of the seed in the soil to gain strength and wisdom from earthly experience, so that the divine seed may grow into the tree of eternal life. As we meditate on this, let us feel that we *are* the seed growing into the tree; let us feel the nourishment being drawn up from the roots embedded in the earth, our physical life, and carried up through the stem into the branches and

leaves. Feel the soft rain falling on the opening leaves; breathe in the lovely scent of the rain and the earth, of the freshened plant life all around; feel the leaves and then the flowers unfolding in the warm, caressing sunlight. The petals of our souls open to the glorious celestial world, where angels of light minister to us.

We lose all sense of separation, and in simple adoration worship the sun, source of our life, and the great mother, soul of the world.

After a short period of utter peace and stillness in this heavenly consciousness, we must make the effort to withdraw—to come down to earth again. Take several gentle but deep breaths and firmly return to the everyday world. It is strange how small and confined the ordinary consciousness feels as we come back to it. Don't forget to 'seal' yourself, as described at the end of the previous chapter, if you feel that you have for a brief time been released into the light.

## Evening meditation

On Monday evening from sunset onwards the angels of Venus are linked with the Moon. This is because the Moon is exalted in the fixed earth sign of Taurus, which is also the negative sign of Venus. This is a powerful combination, particularly helpful for meditation and for work on the etheric plane. The angels of the earth are very much concerned with the etheric world and with the angelic life of nature. The Monday evening meditation in the Essene Brotherhood was upon the angel of peace, which seems especially appropriate for this beautiful Moon–Venus combination. Only when the business and turmoil of everyday thoughts are still can our souls build the etheric bridge into the inner world of light. Again quiet, steady breathing will help to still the thoughts and after the tense activity of the day you will find it specially helpful to concentrate for a few minutes on relaxing the neck and shoulders. Perform the movements slowly and gently, thinking of the star and quietly breathing in the light. You are breathing it into your heart-chakra which is beginning to glow with light as if a beautiful jewel there is reflecting back the rays of light and becoming brighter and brighter.

In this heart-consciousness you feel that you have become one with the star. If you continue peacefully, quietly breathing in the light, you may feel that your soul is opening under the star like the water-lily or lotus, white and fragrant. The jewel in the lotus radiates light. You feel the presence in you and with you of the great healer and draw into this shining jewel of light anyone whom you know needs healing, any condition which you know needs harmonising. The angel of peace enfolds both you and those you long to help in strong and beautiful wings of light.

Before settling to sleep again consciously relax. Think of this angel filling your being with peace and strength, and include in your affirmation the words, 'Divine peace permeates my whole being. I am divine peace'.

## TUESDAY  *The day of Mars*

### *Morning meditation*

The positive or 'day' sign* of Mars is the fiery Aries, exaltation of the Sun, so the angels of this day are those of energy, of industry, of joy in creative achievement. Aries is the sign of the upsurging life and joy of springtime, the vitality and idealism of youth. Its vibrations awaken creative fire in the soul so the meditation for this day is connected with the angels of fire. The fire is the fire of divine love upspringing in the heart, but unless the fire element is directed and controlled by the spirit, it can flare out as anger, temper, irritation and rebellion. Moreover, the energy and enthusiasm of Mars will easily make us feel rather tense in our aspiration. So on this day let us hold in our thoughts the still, clear flame of divine love. Using the relaxing exercise, make sure that head, neck and shoulders are perfectly poised. Breathe gently and peacefully and visualise once again just above the head the shining star of the greater self, with the stream of light pouring down through the top of the head, down the spine and into every cell of the body with each in-breath.

* In the old textbooks, the planets are described as having 'diurnal' and 'nocturnal thrones'. Except in the cases of Venus and Saturn, these signs are the same as the 'positive' and 'negative' signs of present-day astrology.

As you breathe out, feel a light and radiance pouring from the heart-chakra in love and blessing, first to all those in your immediate environment whom it is your duty to love and serve, and then to the wider community, to your nation, then to the world itself. Try to maintain this concentration for seven deep, gentle breaths, becoming with each one more conscious of the still white flame within the heart, burning steadily and brightly. Continuing the deep breathing, now focus your attention on this flame, which draws your aspirations heavenward. Gradually you feel that your whole being is absorbed into the clear flame. You become aware that it is not small or separate but a part of the sun. The flame of your spirit is united with the flame in the hearts of all men. You are one with a shining company of souls, a brotherhood working together with one purpose, to bring light, love and healing to humanity. All have the will to will the will of God. The flames in this great heart are full of joy and exultation, and of a divine energy that makes you want to pour forth praises in song or in dancing, or in practical service on the physical plane. You can fight the good fight on the mental plane with a constant radiation of positive, loving thought. As you finish the meditation remember anyone who is sad and despondent, and try to uphold them with divine love and courage. Then firmly come back to earth.

## Evening meditation

On Tuesday evening from sunset onwards the angels of Mars are linked with those of Saturn. Mars is exalted in Capricorn, the cardinal earth sign which is also the negative sign of Saturn. This is a stern planetary combination, for both Mars and Saturn are traditionally known as malefics, but they strengthen the will-power and bring to this evening's meditation an element of dedication and purposeful direction. A preliminary period of relaxation is specially necessary. Listening to peaceful music could help to release the mind from the cares and responsibilities of the day.

The symbol of Capricorn is the mountain goat, the creature who climbs the heights. The combination of the angels of Mars and Saturn stimulates within the soul the urge to climb to the heights even though the way be hard and dangerous, and the soul has the determination to cope courageously with all difficulties—to raise itself out of the turmoil of the lower self into the spheres of light.

Let us then think of the grandeur and solitude of the mountain heights. We rise slowly in consciousness to the summit of the mountain; we feel the clear, cold, sparkling air; we see the majestic panorama of mountain peaks all round, and in the silence we kneel to worship the Creator. As we worship in this high, lonely place, we feel the light of a radiant star pouring upon us, flooding the neighbouring peaks with light and colour. Beside us is the still form of a great angel, like a pillar of flame, filling us with strength and resolution. We look up into the star and realise that we are clothed in the armour of light. As we breathe in we are given the courage and the will to perform the tasks which lie before us. On our knees we give thanks to the Great White Spirit for his strength and sustenance. The affirmation for this night is 'I am divine strength. Divine strength flows through every fibre of my being. I can and I will overcome all weakness and inharmony through the strength of God in me'.

## WEDNESDAY  *The day of Mercury*

### *Morning meditation*

The positive or 'day' sign of Mercury is the airy Gemini, the heavenly twins, sign of communication and expression. Mercury, as far as we know at present, is the planet closest to the sun and the quickest in motion. Its influence is subtle and elusive, so much so that at humanity's present state of development very few people can fully make use of the qualities he brings. Being so close to the sun he represents the solar body of man gradually taking form, thought by thought, from the substance of pure spirit. The mercurial body of man is one of the celestial bodies,

and the angels of Mercury are of the pure gold ray of divine wisdom.

There is a great discrepancy between divine wisdom and its expression through the human intellect. These two aspects are the twins, one mortal, one immortal, who work always together to bring into human life the consciousness of God. Mercury too has always been known as the winged messenger of the gods. He rules the tongue, the shoulders and the hands, all instruments for the expression of the human spirit through physical life. He rules the lungs also, and his sign, Gemini, is an air sign. Breath gives life, and the more we combine correct

54

breathing with quiet concentration on the life of God which is being drawn into the bloodstream, the more will our bodies become perfect instruments of the spirit and so fulfil the purpose of incarnation. Virgo, the 'night' sign of Mercury, is the sign of discrimination, purity and perfection, the sign of the alchemist who searches for the secret of transmuting base metal into fine gold (the human self illumined by the divine).

The tongue and the hands are man's instruments of expression, and give the power to heal, to comfort and to create harmony, or to wound, destroy or even kill. The choice is expressed in the duality of the twins, and its origin is in the mind, ruled by Mercury. The earthly mind is like a mirror. It can be turned towards the sun to reflect light, or it can be turned to reflect the darkness of the earth: the fear and confusion which fill the daily press. The only way to bring the earthly side of Mercury, the mortal twin, under control is through steadfastly turning the mirror of the mind away from earthly darkness towards the light of the great sun, the true self of all mankind.

On Wednesday, Mercury's day, it will be helpful during the working day to ponder on the use we are making of hands and tongue. Is the tongue being used to utter words which are true, kind and helpful, or is it being allowed to waste energy in useless and even harmful chatter? Are the hands being used lovingly in service and the joy of giving, or grudgingly to obtain as much as possible from an earthly employer? If these instruments are dedicated to serving not only God in the heavens but the God in men their use can bring intense joy and satisfaction. The whole day can become a course of meditation.

For this morning's quiet time, however, let us pay special attention to the breathing. Try to feel that with every breath the blood is being charged with the new life of God, and courses round the body in a living stream bringing vitality and healing to every part. Try to forget any aches and pains and know that the God-life flowing through the bloodstream will clear them right away. Having established the rhythm of breathing, think of the heart as a mirror turned towards the sun. Think only of the sun reflected in the facets of the jewel in the heart. Feel the radiance of the sun until you are at one with the source. *I and my Father are one.* Just be still in the heart of the sun. If there is anyone you would like to heal or hold in the protection of the Christ, just sound their name, and feel them with you in the great sun, the heart of Christ.

## *Evening meditation*

If the whole day has been a form of practical meditation, the quiet period will follow naturally. The planet associated with Wednesday evening is the Sun itself. We return to that golden world of light which we found in the morning, but this time with the joyous thought of the approaching period of renewal and refreshment in the world of light. The sun and the stars are in essence the same. As we adjust our breathing, once again we visualise the star of the true self shining above us, its rays of light building round us a circle of protection. We imagine them penetrating every cell of our being, loosening all the little knots and stresses of the day's events, until in our hearts we feel the facets of the jewel beginning to reflect that light. Hold this thought peacefully until you feel that your whole being has been drawn up into the star. Once again we are one with the great sun, radiating light. In the heart of the sun we visualise that beautiful arch through which we shall pass in sleep, and eventually when we leave the physical body in death. Peacefully we go through the archway into the golden world of God.

## THURSDAY *The day of Jupiter*

### *Morning meditation*

Like Mercury, Jupiter represents the freedom which can come when the powers of the mind and the soul are unfolded and brought to fruition. One symbol of this planet is the winged horse, Pegasus, which took the heroes to their objective, bounding across the heavens in a flash. Both Jupiter and Mercury are planets of movement and swift travel, although Mercury is more concerned with the limited travels of everyday affairs, while Jupiter journeys to far places. The old nursery rhyme tells us that Thursday's child has far to go. Jupiter rules the feet, hips and thighs, so physically he is very much concerned with movement. People with Jupiter strongly placed find any restrictions most irksome and soon become rebellious unless they can see good reasons for these. Then they will accept restricting discipline with surprising meekness for they are natural upholders of the law, both manmade and spiritual.

On a Thursday, according to Dr Szekely, the Essene

Brothers meditated on the great angel of water. They were advised to think of water in all its forms, in raindrops, dewdrops, springs, rivers, waterfalls and oceans.

Although Jupiter's 'day' sign is the fiery Sagittarius he also rules the watery Pisces, sign of the seas and oceans, and is exalted in Cancer, sign of the running streams and rivers. In traditional astrology he is called the Greater Benefic, and he brings abundance to his children. Closely associated with the Moon, he works through the soul-life of humanity, expanding the consciousness of higher planes. He is the planet of religion, quickening in the soul the desire to find truth, to become aware of God. He gives the urge to worship, to aspire heavenwards, and to recognise God in all forms of life.

Jupiter's day then is a day to contemplate the works of God; to recognise the divine in every man, flower and beast; to taste God in the food we eat; to recognise the Lord walking among men, shedding the light of his gracious presence in dark places; pouring forth his mercy and compassion on all mankind.

To express in our lives the influence of the angel of Jupiter we need to consider our thoughts and speech and to regard with special kindness and mercy little failings of our companions which could irritate and annoy us were we not living consciously in the presence of the Great Healer.

On Thursday morning, having performed the preliminary ritual of breathing and relaxing, let us try to feel that we are in this peaceful, wonderful loving presence.

We may reach out to the Great Healer in different ways. Always he will be in the heart of the sun or star. We can in imagination walk across the water to him; we can feel ourselves seated among the group of disciples who heard his sermon on the mount. In childlike simplicity we can open heart and mind to his aura of gentleness and divine love. If anything is disturbing us, let us picture ourselves in the boat with him. See him stilling the waves of fear and angry emotion by the power of the divine spirit within and lifting us into divine peace.

The angels of Jupiter bring the soul under the great wings of love and protection. In the stillness, feel these white wings around you, and throughout the day affirm with joy and thankfulness, *Surely goodness and mercy shall follow me all the days of my life: and I will dwell in the house of the Lord for ever.*

*Evening meditation*

At sunset on this evening, the angel of the moon combines her influence with that of Jupiter. The Moon, the great mother, in whose sign of Cancer Jupiter is exalted, presides over that soul-world into which we withdraw in sleep. Our symbol for meditation is traditionally the lotus bud lying on a still pool, slowly opening its pure white petals under the light of the shining star. In the golden heart of the lotus lies the jewel. In this wonderfully still vibration, the angels of peace draw close to lift the soul into consciousness of the heavenly places.

Filled with deep peace and confidence in God we make the affirmation, 'I am divine love. Divine love always has met and always will meet every human need'. Make this affirmation a number of times as you are dropping asleep and as surely as you do so you will be lifted above all earthly worries into the temple of wisdom in the heaven world, where you will find eternal truth.

## FRIDAY  *The day of Venus*

### *Morning meditation*

Venus is traditionally known as the Lesser Benefic. It seems strange, then, that to the superstitious mind Friday is an unlucky day, and specially to be feared should it fall on the thirteenth of the month.

For Christians Friday is inevitably linked with the crucifixion of Jesus and this is probably one reason for the superstition. Yet the crucifixion is also an occasion for joy, in the orthodox church. Astrologically, the symbolism is a little more general. Venus is the planet associated with love, and with our human relationships generally, as well as with money and possessions; in other words, with objects with which we form emotional attachments. The natural concomitants of love and desire are not only joy in fulfilment but also sadness and pain of separation, denial or loss. Through the whole day we have this emphasis on the balance of joy and pain in the life.

The 'day' sign of Venus is Libra, the cardinal air sign in which Saturn is exalted—Saturn the lord of karma, who metes out exact justice. He upholds the law of brotherhood, which states that we are responsible for the happiness of others and should behave to them as we would like them to behave to us.

When Libra is emphasised in the personal horoscope, it gives an almost instinctive understanding of the way other people are feeling and thinking. It is an air sign, strengthening the reason and ability to give dispassionate judgment, enabling the soul clearly to see both sides of the situation. For this reason Librans are often in trouble and find themselves at the centre of conflict. They long for peace and harmony and are happy so long as the people around them are happy, but the conflict of strong personalities in their environment, especially conflict between those they love, can shatter them, nervously and emotionally. In matters of love and friendship this sign often brings sadness through rivalry. It almost seems as if the beautiful rose of love which Venus represents has to have sharp thorns as well as a heavenly fragrance.

As previously stated, the cross within the circle symbolises the conflict of the elements within man, and is also the symbol of Earth. Venus is the ruler of Taurus, the sign of fixed earth. Perhaps of all the days of the week Friday is the most appropriate one for meditating upon this beautiful symbol of the crucifixion of the soul in matter.

There could be a slightly tense feeling with this influence, so let us concentrate for a few minutes on performing the relaxation and breathing routine. As we do so, gently and slowly, let us try to imagine that we are inhaling the perfume of a lovely rose. Do not try to visualise it at first but just absorb the feeling of its fragrance and sweetness, as if it were resting in your heart and gradually opening to the morning sun. The petals have rain or dewdrops on them, like human tears, which sparkle in the sunlight. Feel the warmth of the sun from above drawing forth the fragrance from the rose as the petals gently unfold. Make no mental effort to see it, but feel in your heart that it is part of your very being. Feel the warmth of the sun pouring down as you breathe in the gentle fragrance. Gradually your rose will become very real to you. You will become aware of its colour, probably different on different days, sometimes a soft pink, sometimes a deep red, or flame, or gold or white. As you become practised in your meditation different colours will bring to your heart a particular quality of consciousness which you are needing. Train yourself to be absolutely still and peaceful in this consciousness of the rose in your heart. Gradually you will become aware that the rose is blooming at the heart of an equal-sided cross of light upon which you are stretched, while the shining circle of God's love enfolds you. Feel, through the rose in your heart, the peace of surrender, of acceptance of all the conditions, the sorrows, the joys, the frustrations and the triumphs which form the cross of your personality. Withdraw from the conflict of the outer self into the heart of the rose and you will begin to feel the divine breath of the Comforter. Be still and absorb the blessing of divine peace and acceptance. ‐

After a little time bring yourself firmly back into physical consciousness in the way described. Then go to your daily tasks carrying with you the feeling of divine love flowing through your heart, enabling you to accept with tranquillity whatever comes.

### Evening meditation

The planet blending with Venus at sunset on a Friday is Mars, whose 'night' sign is Scorpio, associated with the eighth house—with death of the physical body and ultimately with complete surrender of the little human personality to the greater self. This does not mean complete negation or loss of the individuality, as so many people fear, but rather the soul's surrender of all foolish, separative self-will to that glorious, sublime law of God; the law which holds the stars and planets in their courses, which orders night and day and the cycle of the seasons, which brings forth form from the invisible world and withdraws it again when the cycle is complete. So on Friday evening let us meditate on the eternal life of God manifesting ever more completely in a form beautifully adapted as an instrument for the spirit. The symbol of eternal life is the

shining flame which burns in every human heart. Let us then withdraw from the turmoil of the outer world into the innermost temple of our being, where burns this divine flame. We kneel before the altar, fastening our whole attention on the inexhaustible strength and beauty of the flame. Gradually it seems as though the whole altar burns with light. We feel that our whole being is gradually absorbed into the cleansing, immortalising power of this flame. All desire, all ambition, all self-will is consumed by the clear flame of God, the I AM within. Be still, and feel that with the flame you are lifted into the heart of the great sun temple of universal brotherhood where all are united in the one flame; that you are united with every other human heart. Upon the flame the grace of heavenly love pours down, as the human brotherhood is united with that of the spheres and planetary angels, so that all become part of a great star in the heavens.

Before going to sleep, think of this glorious, blazing star and repeat the affirmations, *I and my Father are one Father, into thy hands I commend my spirit.*

## SATURDAY    *The day of Saturn*

### *Morning meditation*

Saturn's number is eight, the number of a perfect cube, 2 × 2 × 2, and Saturn is essentially the planet of perfection in form. His work in the universal plan is to purify and perfect form so that it becomes an ever more worthy instrument of the spirit. He is often symbolised as the great reaper, Old Father Time, with his hour-glass and scythe. Just as time tests the quality of material objects and arrangements, so Saturn tests and perfects those soul-qualities which will be used ultimately in the creation of man's solar body, the temple of the sun.

To work with the angel of Saturn, we should regard Saturday as a special day for dispassionate self-assessment. The Essene Brotherhood encouraged its members on one day of the week to make a survey of their actions and reactions throughout the past seven days, noticing calmly where they had failed, where they had been slothful in their habits, harsh in their judgments of others, or blind to creative opportunity. This summary of the week's activity was done not in a miserable or guilty way, but calmly and dispassionately, taking note of facets of the nature which required improvement. This is common practice also with yogis. Having made the assessment, it is foolish to feel excessively remorseful. We are all learning lessons in earth's school, working through tests and exercises. The result of the Saturday assessment should be an acceptance of the situation. Then with prayer and patient endeavour, we set the God-will within us working to perfect the deficiencies which we have noted.

Socrates held that self-control is an exact science. We can learn it through the regular practice of meditation and through our nightly affirmations. As we survey the meditations for the different days of the week, together with the lesson of our own Sun-sign, it should not be difficult to discover what needs improving in ourselves and in our daily contacts.

The positive sign of Saturn is Aquarius, sign of friendship and brotherhood, and it will probably be our shortcomings in our relationships with those about us that need most prayer and endeavour. Jesus summed up the whole of the law and the prophets in the words, *Thou shalt love the Lord thy God with all thy heart, and with all thy soul, and with all thy strength, and with all thy mind; and thy neighbour as thyself.*

Saturn is the slowest of the seven traditional planets and one of his principles is perseverance. In this weekly assessment it is best not to set our sights too high but to find just one area in which we can become braver, wiser, kinder and more positive. All of us fail in many ways, and if we can put right just one thing which causes trouble to family or workmates, let us work on this until it is corrected.

Calm recognition of our imperfections, willing the will of God in our thoughts and affirmations, will help us gradually to build the perfect soul-temple—the temple of the sun. Having made our assessment let us kneel in deep silence before the altar, in the temple of our innermost being and feel the light from above pouring down upon us, giving strength to realise our resolution.

It is interesting that Saturn presides over the New Year when we lightly make resolutions. If we can ponder upon these resolutions on Saturn's day each week and allow the God-will to move us, we shall make steady progress towards the New Jerusalem of the book of Revelation where the perfected soul of humanity is symbolised in the perfect cube.

## *Evening meditation*

The planetary ruler for sunset on a Saturday is Mercury. Its negative or 'night' sign is Virgo, associated with the sixth house, the house of service and of health. When following the path of meditation there is a danger of falling into the habit of thinking only of one's own spiritual unfoldment and progress, but these Saturday meditations are a regular reminder that as we become increasingly aware of the light, the God, within our own being, that light must be allowed to radiate in loving service to all life. The light shines in darkness. As the 'nocturnal throne' of Saturn is Aquarius, sign of universal brotherhood and friendship, the message to be understood is that the world will gradually draw together into a family of nations happy in the serene and loving guidance of the

Father–Mother God.

When Saturn and Mercury are harmoniously aspected in a natal chart, they give splendid powers of concentration and philosophic thought, and so the combination of these two, which occurs on a Saturday evening, makes a particularly good occasion for the radiation of light and healing, not only to individuals but to conditions of turmoil and unrest throughout the world. Since Virgo is the sign of service and healing, let us co-operate with the angels of Mercury and Saturn by focusing our thought-power in service for the healing of the nations.

So, for our meditation, having become relaxed and poised under the star, let us take seven deep breaths, and with each one become filled with light. Take only three if you are not used to this deep breathing. Now, breathing peacefully and gently, let us picture a shining jewel in the heart-chakra. Hold it absolutely still under the star. See nothing but the glorious, blazing star pouring its light upon the jewel, which begins to shine and sparkle and to radiate light from every facet. Turn this shining diamond about under the blazing light and see it becoming brighter and more powerful, a myriad facets of flashing light and colour. In its very heart is a radiant white centre. Feel the stillness and power of this centre, then say the name of any person, condition or country you want to help or serve. Do not for one moment take your attention off the still, white centre of the starlit jewel but from deep within your heart, sound the name. If you cannot say it aloud, whisper it or mouth the syllables so that you bring the name into your physical consciousness without any break in your concentration on the light. After saying each name, rest peacefully under the star for a few moments before passing on to the next name.

When you have finished this radiation, peacefully surrender your whole being to the light. Feel that you are kneeling in absolute stillness and acceptance as the light from above pours down, cleansing you, burning up all thought of self, until you can say from your deepest heart, *I and my Father are one.*

Before sleep, again let the affirmation be, 'The Christ Star shines in my heart, permeating, illumining every cell of my being—*I and my Father are one*'.

SUNDAY  *The day of the Sun*

*Morning meditation*

The old nursery rhyme tells that 'The child that's born on the Sabbath day Is fair and wise and good and gay'. This certainly describes the sunny temperament possessed by people strongly under the solar ray. The vibrations of this day are naturally happy and positive, for the Sun in the horoscope is associated with the fifth house, of pleasure, entertainment, happy relaxation with children; the house of lovers, and of recreation of all kinds. In fact creation and recreation, and all joyous activity, are the natural expression of the life of the Sun, both in man and in nature.

It is sad that religious observance tends in all faiths to become so formalised that the participants lose the joyous sense of restoration of soul and spirit which praise and worship of God should bring. Worship of the Creator could pour forth from the heart as joyfully as the song of the lark on a spring morning, for if we worship truly we cannot but feel in our hearts the upspringing of new life.

Dr Szekely tells us in his book that for the Essenes the midnight communion marked the beginning of the new day. Their Saturday-night communion was with the angel of eternal life, whom we may regard as the great angel of the sun. The sun is the giver of life to all the different bodies of man, from the physical to the celestial or solar. The sun's light streams into the earth, generating the life of grass and plant and tree; generating all animal life, all human life. Meditation under the wings of the angel of the sun can fill the soul with new life and joy and strength, nourishing and sustaining it in all its different vehicles.

From the solar body the vitality of the sun flows constantly through the physical body by means of the bloodstream, which is recharged with every breath.

In all our meditations we can be much helped by a conscious regulation of the breath, but on Sunday, the day of the restoration of the soul, of the eventual resurrection of the body, a conscious breathing-in of the vitality of the sun can be specially helpful. It is worth giving extra time to it and enjoying it. Try to picture the sun rising over a still sea (representing your soul). Feel the warmth of the sun's rays; see the shining path which it makes across the water and feel that you are being drawn along this path. You are walking on the surface of the water, following the golden pathway right into the sun. Do not strain in any way, either in the breathing or the visualising, but feel your whole being opening in praise and adoration. Feel in your heart the wonder of the mighty, creative power of the universe and feel with the Psalmist that with your whole being you want to *sing unto the Lord a new song; for he hath done marvellous things*. Let the mind and body be still, relaxed and at peace, and rest in the glory of this sun-consciousness. Feel it revitalising and restoring every cell of your being, filling you with loving kindness for all creation. Sound the great OM in your heart and realise your unity with every living thing. St Francis of Assisi's song of the creatures beautifully expresses the vibrations of this holy day.

Such prayer and meditation on the day of rest and re-creation will have an increasingly beneficial effect on both your physical health and the harmony of your life.

## Evening meditation

The planetary angel blending with the Sun's from sunset onwards is that of Jupiter, planet of the higher mind, the planet which helps us to grow the wings of our spirit. It is interesting that this planet which governs religion, philosophy and worship, holds sway at a time so often associated with religious services, for it is a specially helpful influence in raising the consciousness of the participants. Even if they cannot respond fully to the beautiful vibrations they will generally be aware of the specially peaceful quality of most evening services.

Jupiter is the planet of freedom and expansion, also of aspiration to heavenly wisdom. The Sunday evening meditation reinforces the joyous recreation of the morning. The so-called 'night' sign of Jupiter is Pisces, sign of the great oceans and the life therein. The symbol of the fish swimming in the ocean and absorbing life from it shows how the human soul can be restored and healed by its immersion in the great ocean of cosmic life. Meditation on the power within the sea and on the life-giving qualities of water helps us to become attuned to the great mother of life from whom we all draw sustenance. On this holy day of the sun we can be revitalised by the divine fire of the Father while our souls are cleansed and restored by the angels of water, angels of the Divine Mother.

After focusing the thoughts quietly on the strength of the sea, let us contemplate any of the Christian parables, which show the Master's control of this element. In imagination again we look across the waves towards the setting sun, seeing them become ever more still, and watch them reflect the glory and the colour of sunset. With the Master we enter the boat of the soul and glide towards the heart of the sun, into the golden world of God, to which we will shortly withdraw during sleep.

As we settle for the night, let us consciously relax every part of the body, starting at the toes, stretching and relaxing each set of joints and muscles right up to the crown of the head. Before dropping asleep, we speak the affirmation, 'Divine life shines in my heart; divine life renews and restores every cell of my being. I AM the resurrection and the life'. This will help you during the night to be free of the physical environment and, like the fish in the cosmic ocean, to be recharged with divine light.

*

Since the position of the Sun in the birth-chart shows the particular soul-vehicle which is being vivified through everyday experience, it seems that the day of the week whose planet rules the Sun-sign should bring particularly helpful vibrations for meditation and spiritual unfoldment. Thus, those born under Sagittarius, whose ruler is Jupiter, should find Thursday a specially useful day. The number of the day of birth, when reduced to a single digit (the total of its digits, i.e. $22 = 2 + 2 = 4$), is also associated with a particular planet and day which will be important in the life.

These rulerships are as follows.

MONDAY: planet, Moon; numbers, 2 and 7. Significant for those born between June 22 and July 23* when the Sun was in Cancer, or on the 2nd, 11th and 20th or the 7th, 16th and 25th of any month.

TUESDAY: planet, Mars; number, 9. Significant for those born with Sun in Aries (March 21–April 20) and Scorpio

* The dates of each sign vary slightly from year to year. For convenience, those of a typical year in the middle of this century have been chosen.

(October 24–November 22) or on 9th, 18th or 27th of any month.

WEDNESDAY: planet, Mercury; number, 5. Significant for those born with Sun in Gemini (May 21–June 22) and Virgo (August 23–September 23), or on the 5th, 14th or 23rd of any month.

THURSDAY: planet, Jupiter; number 3. Significant for those born with Sun in Sagittarius (November 22–December 22) and Pisces (February 19–March 21), or on the 3rd, 12th, 21st or 30th of any month.

FRIDAY: planet, Venus; number, 6. Significant for those born with Sun in Taurus (April 22–May 22) and Libra (September 23–October 24), or on the 6th, 15th or 24th of any month.

SATURDAY: planet, Saturn; number, 8. Significant for those born with Sun in Capricorn (December 22–January 21) and Aquarius (January 21–February 19), or on the 8th, 17th or 26th of any month.

SUNDAY: planet, Sun; numbers, 1 and 4. Significant for those born with Sun in Leo (July 23–August 23), or on the 1st, 10th, 19th, 28th, or the 4th, 13th, 22nd or 31st of any month.

*

## The Extra-Saturnian Planets

### Uranus

The three extra-Saturnian planets have not been included in this weekly rhythm because their spiritual vibrations are so subtle that we will only begin to feel them, if at all, when we have made some progress in our awareness of the seven traditional planets. The vibrations of Uranus can only be truly understood by the soul who has progressed quite considerably under the ray of Saturn, until he is fully aware of, and tries lovingly to fulfil, his responsibility in family relationships, to his employer, to his country, to the spiritual group to which he belongs. The rays of Uranus are to be felt through deep brotherhood of the spirit and in forms of group service. The man ready to respond to Uranus will be beginning to master his own thoughts and emotions and will be growing steadily more at one with the divinity within.

The number of Uranus is four, which previously was given to the Sun. Probably the master-number, twenty-two, rather than four, will give numerologists a key to the vibrations of this planet. People born on the 4th, 13th, 22nd and 31st of any month have some affinity with Uranus, and Sunday will be a significant day for them. We might almost regard both Saturday *and* Sunday as Uranian days, for both hold before us the ideal of man-made-perfect, the Sun-man in whom the divine fire of the spirit irradiates the physical body, and whose whole life is lived in brotherhood.

## *Neptune*

The number of Neptune is seven, which is also traditionally associated with the Moon. People born on the 7th, 16th or 25th of any month will to some extent respond to the magical vibrations of this planet, though they will more likely feel the influence of the Moon, and Monday will be for them a significant day. The jewels, colours and herbs of the Moon will also apply to them. Neptune is the planet of mystery and of psychic awareness. His subtler vibrations can only be touched in meditation by those who have learned to still the demands of the emotions and the outer personality. Neptune is also linked with Jupiter through his rulership of Pisces, and the Sunday-evening meditation leading into the Moonday is a time when those sufficiently sensitive could be caught up for a few moments into the cosmic consciousness which he represents.

## *Pluto*

The number allotted to Pluto is eleven, the 'one' of the new series of numbers beginning from ten—which is interesting, because he is always associated with a fresh start, the beginning of a new cycle of experience. Pluto certainly seems to have a close association with the eighth house and with Scorpio, with death and regeneration. His vibrations are only touched when we die small deaths within our own being, when we experience a crucifixion of the lower self. Such losses help to prepare us for that major experience of the Second Death, the surrender of all personal attachments and desires, which must come to every soul. The Second Death releases man from the limitations of the lower personality and leads to the freedom and glorious joy of the Resurrection. Because of Pluto's close link with the crucifixion of the lower self and with Scorpio, we would link him with Friday, the day when Christ himself was crucified.

# 7

## The Cycle of the Months and the Years

Although religious observance takes many and various outward forms, the oldest of all religions is Sun-worship. Properly understood, this is part of the ancient wisdom which has persisted since the earth came into being. Occult teaching states that the ancient wisdom was brought to the earth by the Sun-men, souls who have advanced far beyond the comprehension of even the most powerful human intelligence, and also that great Sun-beings have in their charge every cycle of evolving human souls. Time, as we know it, does not exist in the cosmos, and even the finest human brain is as a candle to the sun, in comparison both with the time-scale of which these cycles are only the parts and with the consciousness of these Sun-men.

The Sun-beings demonstrated the cosmic and universal law by which man must live in order to attain to mastery. Their knowledge extended to the relation of the cycles of evolution to the cosmic whole. It is believed that the symbols of this knowledge are now buried beneath the oceans and the desert sands, and only fragments of it remain in the outer symbols of the religious festivals in different lands. Most of the religions have festivals linked with the apparent path of the sun through the heavens, and with the gifts of the seasons, out of which man receives the necessities for his life on earth. Astrologically, all these festivals relate to the hidden influence of the Sun in the different signs of the zodiac, and thus to the development of the heavenly consciousness of man.

75

Every religion also has its great teachers, souls who have progressed so far on the path of spiritual unfoldment that they are able to perform miracles of healing, to raise souls from apparent death, and to demonstrate their mastery over the physical atoms by walking on the water, stilling storms, changing water into wine.

The twelve signs which are the basis of so much religious symbolism divide naturally into four groups of three, under the elements fire, earth, air and water, or into three groups of four, according to the quality, or mode of manifestation, known as cardinal, fixed and mutable.

These qualities are closely linked with the four seasons. The Sun enters the four cardinal signs (Aries, Cancer, Libra and Capricorn) at the seasonal turning-points, the equinoxes and the solstices. Each of these signs ushers in a different phase of activity in nature, and in man a different outlook, with fresh plans to be made, fresh ideas to be worked out for the coming season.

The cardinal signs symbolise action, power and energy. They represent the will-aspect of the Trinity, which brings to the soul the urge for incarnation, for action and for earthly experience. These will eventually lead to complete mastery of spirit over matter. Fittingly, then, the sun-festivals of the equinoxes and solstices are the most outstanding in the year and symbolise the incarnation of the spirit or Christ in matter, the battles which, fought to ultimate victory, will bring forth a 'new heaven and a new earth'.

The solstice-festivals of Christmas and Midsummer celebrate the birth and destiny of Christ, the sun-spirit, or the Son of God, through incarnation in matter, while the equinoctial festivals, known in the Christian church as Easter and the feast of St Michael and all angels, symbolise the testing and crucifixion of the spirit in matter, and its ultimate triumph when it has learnt the law of balance between light and darkness, good and evil, spirit and matter.

The changing seasons are due to the tilt of the earth's axis, and we find the cycle symmetrically opposite in the northern and southern hemispheres, so that Spring in the one corresponds with Autumn or Fall in the other. This constant alternation demonstrates to man the omnipresence and omnipotence of the great spirit of the sun, for

in the sun-cycle or circle is no beginning and no end, and every ending coincides with a new beginning. Spring in the North is autumn in the South, birth into the physical consciousness is like death to the soul, and death of the physical body is rebirth into the life of spirit. The spiral of life is eternal and ever-progressing. Participants in the ancient sun-ceremonies walked in spiral procession up to the hilltop temples to receive blessing from the outpouring of the Solar Logos.

The fixed signs (Taurus, Leo, Scorpio and Aquarius) show another and quite different aspect of the Godhead: they are all concerned with consolidation, stabilisation, organisation. They represent the practical manifestation of the phases of life, the seasons; the ideas or the projects which the cardinal signs have originated. All the fixed signs are concerned with human feelings, with possessions and security on all planes of being, and thus demonstrate the love-aspect of the Trinity. Love is building or creating with Light. The religious festivals connected with these signs might be called festivals of comfort, for they bring a realisation of the eternal goodness and mercy of God through life and death. The Buddhist Wesak festival, celebrated when the Sun is in Taurus, and the festivals of All Saints and All Souls, and in latter days Remembrance Sunday, when the Sun is in Scorpio, help to bring home to those imprisoned in the flesh the reality of the life of spirit, and to show how thin is the veil which separates the earthly from the heavenly consciousness. The fixed quality of the signs demonstrates the infinite patience and steadfastness needed to tread the path leading to full spiritual realisation. The path lies not through the intellect, not through concentrated action, but through the heart and the feelings; feelings which have been engendered by human action and reaction, and which gradually teach the soul an infinite compassion and a sense of responsibility towards brother man and his needs. The festivals of the fixed signs are also closely related to the inner life, the life of feeling, emotion and intuition. When the Sun passes through the Leo–Aquarius polarity we have Candlemas, or the festival of the Lights, in February, and in August that of the Transfiguration, when Jesus demonstrated the power of the inner light to transform the physical atoms. Both these festivals remind the soul of the constant and unfailing power of the light within the heart of every man to guide, succour and illumine him on his pathway through matter, until he attains to Christhood, when comes the transmutation of all the physical atoms. The Moon, symbol of the soul of mankind, is exalted in the fixed earth sign of Taurus, showing how vital is the experience of physical life to soul-development.

Thus, while the cardinal or action-signs, Aries, Cancer, Libra and Capricorn, represent the will of the spirit to incarnate and through crucifixion to attain resurrection, the fixed-signs of Taurus, Leo, Scorpio and Aquarius represent the building of the permanent soul-temple—an immortalised physical body.

The mutable signs (Gemini, Virgo, Sagittarius and Pisces) represent the third or wisdom-aspect of the Trinity. The Sun passes through these signs when each season has passed its peak and nature is beginning to show signs of coming change. These signs symbolise flexibility, adaptability and the garnering of wisdom through experience.

While the Sun is in Gemini the Christian festival of Whitsun occurs, which is linked with the Christ-festival at the time of the June full Moon. At this time there is a great spiritual outpouring which quickens the higher consciousness of those prepared to receive it. In the Christian story the disciples, after their love had been most severely tested, were by arrangement gathered in an upper room. In other words, they were raised in consciousness as a group to receive the Christ-baptism. This was seen as tongues of flame above their heads, and by this divine fire they were illumined. All their latent spiritual gifts were awakened, and henceforth they were filled with the power of the spirit to work so-called miracles.

Three out of the four mutable signs, namely Gemini, Sagittarius and Pisces, are known as double-bodied signs, and represent the duality of man's consciousness—his

earthly or frontal mind and the higher or deeper consciousness which belongs to his real and eternal self, and is
built of the experience of many lives—the part of him
which can soar on the wings of the spirit and creative
imagination far above earth-limitations. They also symbolise the balancing of the two opposing forces which
man has to learn to understand and bring under his control. They all symbolise in different ways the immortality
and freedom of the human spirit. Mercury, ruler of

Gemini, and Jupiter, ruler of Sagittarius, both have wings
as part of their symbolism—in the winged sandals of
Mercury, and the winged horse Pegasus, steed of Jupiter
in Greek mythology, the spirit learns to rise out of earthly
bondage on wings of creative imagination. The Piscean
symbol of the fish which draws its nourishment from the
ocean of universal life again shows how the individual
soul is sustained and immortalised by the divine life-force.

Virgo, the fourth of the wisdom-signs, points the way to
the realisation of union with the cosmic life. It symbolises
the virgin matter, in which the immortal Christ-con-
sciousness is conceived and gradually brought into being

through earthly experience. The Virgin is usually pictured either with a sheaf or an ear of corn in her hand, which partly relates to the physical fact that sowing and harvesting occur when the Sun is passing through the respective periods of the Virgo–Pisces polarity. But the deeper symbolism is the seed of God-consciousness, which is sown into the physical life, in which it must grow and mature through human experience. It indicates the sowing and reaping of karma whereby the soul gains heavenly wisdom, discrimination and purity.

Because the development of the soul of man corresponds so closely with the movement of the heavens, we shall find it helpful to link our meditation to some extent with the rhythm of the seasons and the passage of the Sun through the twelve signs of the zodiac. The Sun in the heavens corresponds in a magical way with the heart-centre in the human being, which it rules. According to the position of the Sun in the zodiac at the time of our birth we respond to certain spiritual rays; we feel the influence of certain planetary angels who guide and guard our lives. This influence persists through the whole of an incarnation. Nevertheless, if we can train ourselves to respond to the influences of the Sun's passage through the different signs, and in meditation become a little more aware of the prevailing solar influence, it can be beneficial to our spiritual unfoldment.

The Sun takes a year to travel through all the signs, the Moon only twenty-eight days. She too will affect our passing moods and emotional reactions.

At the time of the full moon each month, when both Sun and Moon are in the same degree of opposite signs there is a special concentration of psychic or soul-force. The full moon has always been recognised as a time specially important for magical practice and spiritual work. The pull of opposing forces from the complementary signs at this time brings an increase of psychic tension, which produces marked effects in certain types of mental illness. It seems to sensitise the nervous system, especially in people who are in any way already psychic, making it more difficult for them to remain poised and at peace, and yet sometimes bringing a beautiful illumination of consciousness to those who manage to rise in spirit beyond the spheres of conflict.

At the new moon, when the Sun and Moon are in the same degree of the same sign of the zodiac, there is a concentration of power which gives a special opportunity for starting fresh enterprises. The new moon, no matter in what sign of the zodiac it occurs, is always symbolic of a fresh beginning, a rebirth. The period between the new and the full moon is a time of rising sap, when all the natural forces are as it were working up to a full tide. The actual new moon occurs a day or two before we joyfully see that little slip of a moon shining in the western sky soon after sunset. The actual new moon is invisible for it occurs when the moon is between the earth and the sun and cannot reflect the latter's light to the earth.

Because at this time the Moon and Sun are in exactly the same degree of the same sign the power of that sign is intensified, and even more so if an eclipse occurs. As we become more sensitive to the tides of spiritual force and to the angels of the elements we shall be able to attune ourselves in our meditations to the prevailing astrological influence. When the sign in which the new moon falls is in any way emphasised in an individual's birth-chart, the soul will be particularly responsive to it and should be able to find a special recharging of their spirit in meditation. Symbolically, a new moon indicates the soul withdrawing from all earthly interests and turning inward to the great sun temple for renewal. In just the same way we seek refreshment in sleep when our souls turn away from all outward activities and we withdraw into our own inner world.

As the age of Aquarius advances, bringing deeper knowledge of spiritual as well as physical science, man will become increasingly aware of the power and beauty of these rhythmic sun–moon-festivals and will learn to attune himself to them. Whatever part of the world he inhabits, he will learn how to rise on the wings of his spirit to the universal temple of the sun, and to hear in his soul the celestial harmonies. He will beat with the stars and planets and all nature the rhythm of the eternal dance of joy and thanksgiving.

In the following chapters we shall study the inner significance of the full moons, taking them in pairs as they occur when the Sun and Moon are in the same degree of complementary signs, and of the new moons, taking them singly as they occur when Sun and Moon are in the same sign.

# 8

## The Moons of the Cardinal Cross

### The Cancer Capricorn Moon Cycle

#### The full moons

Let us first consider the full Moons occurring in the solstice signs, Cancer and Capricorn. When the Sun is in Capricorn (between December 22 and January 21 each year), the full Moon will be in Cancer, and when the Sun is in Cancer (between June 22 and July 23), the full Moon will be in Capricorn.

The angels of the Moon and Saturn, the planets ruling the solstice signs, are the angels of time and tide, those powerful angels of form which govern man's life in the physical body. The angels of the Moon, at the head of which is the archangel Gabriel, are the angels of birth and motherhood; while the angels of Saturn, under the archangel Cassiel (or Jophiel), have the task of shaping and disciplining matter into perfect form, bringing law and order out of chaos. We may also think of Saturn as the great gardener with his pruning shears, cutting away unwanted branches so that the trees will grow more vigorously according to their own perfect pattern. Yet because even perfection implies limitation, the cycle of growth is unending. Spirit is beyond form, and uses it as an instrument, a truth which is symbolised at each solstice.

The solstices mark the seasonal high and low watermarks of the tides of natural life. Both in June and December, from about the 19th to the 23rd of the month, the sun appears to stand still in its journey north or south

of the equator. It pauses for about three days before starting its journey back. It is this time of stillness which gives
the solstice its name—the standing-still of the sun.
During this period, if we allow ourselves to withdraw
from the distractions of the outer world, we shall become
aware of a deep silence, as if all nature is waiting for
something; then, as the sun turns, on Christmas Eve or at
Midsummer, the little flame of new life, which heralds
another season, comes into being. This tiny flame of eternal life, the immortal flame of spirit, is the Christ-child.
Meditation on this mystery of the rebirth of spirit in form,
on the immortality of spirit and the fluctuating nature of
all form will help us to an understanding of the power
and the wonder of the Christ in man, that true self which,
never dying, ever creates new form.

Another symbol linked with the solstices is that of the
great tree of life, whose roots go down deep into the earth
and whose branches fill the heavens. With unchanging
rhythm the buds break into new life and the tree is
clothed with leaves, flowers and fruit. Then the tide of life
changes, and the sap withdraws; the leaves begin to
wither and fall; the life-forces become dormant. By the
putting forth of fresh foliage every year a great tree is
built from a tiny sapling. In the same way, through the
constant cycle of birth, death and rebirth the spirit, the
seed of God in man, gradually creates the most perfect
form and learns how to immortalise it.

Both Cancer and Capricorn are the signs of home and
family. Christmas is the festival of the family, when we
delight in re-establishing old links. Each family has its
own special rites and ceremonies which the children
expect year after year. It is as if this festival builds up in a
family rather like a great tree, the Christmas tree, which
is at the heart of so many of our Christmas celebrations,
as a symbol of eternal life ever coming into new form but

85

always of the same essence, divine love.

The little family rituals of Christmas mean much to children. For the rest of us if they are performed with understanding and love they help to build a bridge between the world of spirit and the world of form so that a particularly beautiful and loving communion can take place. This 'standing-still' of all the forces of nature demonstrates to humanity the need for silence the need to withdraw from the bustle of the outer rituals and to wait in silent contemplation of the great star in the heavens, shining down on the little human babe and the family in the stable whom the angels of birth, of divine motherhood, enfold in their wings.

At the Summer Solstice, the fragrant rose is another symbol of the Christ-birth and the deep love of the Divine Mother. As we meditate on this, the realisation comes that love is eternal, untouched by change of physical form, and we feel in our hearts the deep happiness of true communion. So with the special outpouring of the heavenly blessing at these times when the Sun stands still; and as we too become still in mind and body angels draw close to help us commune in spirit with those we love— either in the great hall of Christmas in the heaven-world, or in the infinite and eternal garden of the Summerland, where the beautiful roses breathe into our hearts the fragrance of divine love.

## The new moon in Capricorn

The new Moon in Capricorn falls some time between December 22 and January 21 each year, and the Sun and Moon are both in the same degree of this cardinal earth sign, so that the power of the angels of Saturn is particularly felt. Saturn is sometimes equated with Satan, and since he rules the sign of Capricorn, the mountain goat, the horns and cloven hoof of the goat have become

for the superstitious a symbol of evil. Yet the angels of
Saturn have a special work to do in testing, purifying and
strengthening the human soul. Capricorn governs the
tenth house in the horoscope chart, the house of worldly
ambition and social standing, the significance of which is
to develop the down-to-earth side of the nature. The true
Capricornian is extremely practical and hardworking. He
knows exactly what he wants to achieve and the difficulties he must surmount. He possesses a quality of determination and one-pointedness which enables him to
put everything else on one side in order to attain his goal.
His ambition may be on the purely practical plane—in
the business world or in politics; it may be on the mental
plane. Such was the case of Louis Pasteur, who had six
planets in this sign. Because of his slow, methodical way
of working he was considered a dunce at school, but he
plodded on to achieve such mastery of his subject that he
became one of the world's outstanding scientists.

We all need to develop and use Saturn's strength and
will-power. We need the self-discipline and sense of purpose he gives if we are to achieve our goal. But inevitably
as man realises that will-power can achieve almost anything, he experiences the temptations of pride and self-
will. When he has gained a certain amount of knowledge
and practical ability he can over-estimate the power of
the intellect and become self-opinionated. It is this pride
of achievement, both worldly and spiritual, which is
Saturn's deep temptation. When Satan tempted Jesus, we
notice that all the temptations were concerned with the
glorification of the personal self.

This temptation need not be in major concerns. In
daily life we all succumb in small ways to the glorification
of the little self, and wish to appear clever, attractive,
popular. This is where the angels of Saturn can cause the
individual to be separated from the great sun, the glori-

ous, universal eternal self. Yet Capricorn rules the knees, and so the gesture of humility also. At the time the new Moon is in Capricorn it can be helpful in meditation to make a clear-eyed, dispassionate assessment of the strength and weakness of the earthly personality, held so firmly in the grip of karma.

Saturn is the lord of karma, bringing to our minds and bodies the limitations of circumstances and physical equipment which we have earned. When these limitations take the form of some physical handicap, it can strengthen in the soul the qualities of humility and compassion. White Eagle says: 'We suggest that those who suffer—particularly because of blindness or defective vision—may have come to the last step upon a road of soul-cleansing or development. We are too apt to say, "so and so is suffering as the result of karma". This term is used a little loosely. Perhaps it would be more correct to say, "so and so's body is suffering because he, the soul, has reached the end of a certain path of growth or learning which has been undertaken".'*

In THE PATH OF THE SOUL White Eagle tells us that the earth-initiation, which represents the physical life, is the final one, in which the soul has to bring into practical operation the divine creative fire, the secret magic of the adepts.† It is at this stage that the greatest temptation comes to the soul through Saturn or Satan, the temptation to use that trained, developed power of thought for selfish ends. To use it in this way is really black magic, which is often signified by the goat's head—the power of Saturn misused.

But soul-power directed selflessly and dispassionately to awaken and strengthen the Christ light in others is white

* *The Living Word of St John* (White Eagle Publishing Trust, 1979) p. 77.
† (ib., 1959), p. 64.

magic. The soul learning to use white magic will never in any circumstances try to coerce or tempt another, or subject him to his will, nor use this magical power for material gain. So do the angels of Saturn test the soul for its purity of motive and dedication.

Traditionally we make good resolutions on New Year's Eve. Perhaps the new Moon in Capricorn would be a specially powerful time to do this, after meditation on the lesson of one's Sun-sign. Let us think of the particular quality of consciousness in which we are trying to develop through everyday experience and pray for deeper understanding of how this quality can illumine our daily life. In this way we are preparing ourselves for the earth-initiation, the one in which we bring the divine fire into full practical expression, like the birth of the Christ-babe. In the stable is symbolised our material life among the circle of animals (all the astrological types of our companions and the human experiences which our destiny brings us). At the heart of this circle under the star the Christ-babe is born.

Let us then at the time of the new Moon withdraw into the temple of silence in the heart and kneel before the altar with the pure white flame, symbolised by the dot within the circle. The kneeling is important, because only when all pride and self-will is surrendered do we truly fall on our knees before the supreme Light, the source of our being. In silence we pray for clear vision, for strength, humility and patience, the necessary qualities for us to build into our souls the lessons of life's experiences.

### The new moon in Cancer

The new Moon in the sign of Cancer falls some time between June 22 and July 23. The Sun enters the sign at the Summer Solstice, when all the natural forces of life and growth are at their peak. The three days of the Solstice, from about the 19th to the 22nd, correspond with the three days of the Winter Solstice just before Christmas, and are a time of special spiritual outpouring which subtly affects the whole of natural life. Should the new Moon fall close to this solstice-time it will be unusually potent for it will not only be in its own sign but united with the Sun. The water element of Cancer symbolises the soul, the soul of humanity, the soul of nature. It is the sign of the soul-group—the natural group of the family;

the wider group of the community or tribe of which the family is part; the soul of the nation; the soul of the world. As the air element is concerned with the mental body of man, so the water element is concerned with the development of the feelings, the sympathies—the soul. The feelings may be locked entirely in the physical senses, or in the ever-changing moods of the personality; or, as the soul evolves, may expand into the ocean of universal consciousness, the great mother of life in all its forms. This state is not arrived at by any effort of the thinking mind but by the developing response of the feelings to joy and beauty, sorrow and pain.

Being the element of human sympathy and understanding, water is very close to all our human and physical experience. Water and earth blend easily. They can form a stagnant, muddy bog, or can create a joyous, swift-flowing river. So can the soul-consciousness of an individual be blocked in with sensuality or freed to run as a clear stream into the sea of universal consciousness.

The midsummer sign of Cancer has much to do with the life-stream of nature in the myriad plant and animal forms. In the northern hemisphere the life-tide is at its height at this time. It is easy in the physical and emotional pleasure of the long summer days to miss the subtler power of the angelic forces even though Midsummer is traditionally a time for fairy magic. In the northern hemisphere the nature spirits are particularly active, while in the southern hemisphere midwinter passivity heralds the rebirth of a new spring, just as Christmas does in the north.

In meditation at this midsummer time the feelings and emotions must be channelled into stillness. Those who have gardens will be able as they work to attune themselves to the life-force of the great mother, with her angels of form—from the devic beings right down to the little earth-elementals and fairies. These latter are not contacted by thought, but by feeling. You can almost feel them in your hands if you are working with the soil.

All mothers of families need to be practical, and Cancer is a very practical sign; yet even in the practicality there is a sympathetic awareness of the emotional needs of the family. This activity of the feelings may be difficult to control when the sign is emphasised both by the Sun and the Moon, but at the same time it can be used, by those experienced in meditation, to open the soul-consciousness to a most beautiful realisation of divine peace, strength and protection. The meditation on the growth of a seed from its imprisonment in earth to its full blooming as a perfect rose, or as a tall shady tree revelling in the glory of the summer sun, will enable the soul-consciousness to unfold and reach out to the finer, subtler states of life. As we return from such a state of vision beyond words we may well feel that the soul is returning into a tiny box for its daily existence, but there will remain a feeling of unshakeable serenity and well-being. In this way we begin to glimpse the meaning of that peace which passeth all understanding, which the world can neither give nor take away.

## The Aries–Libra Moon Cycle

### The full moons

The full moon of the Spring Equinox, when the Sun is in Aries and the Moon in Libra, is linked with the Easter festival which Christians celebrate on the first Sunday after it. This full moon will occur some time between March 21 and April 20 each year, while that of the Autumn Equinox, when the Sun is in Libra and the Moon in Aries, will occur between September 23 and October 24, quite close to the festival of St Michael and all angels, on September 29 with which it is linked.

As the earth makes its annual journey round the sun, the cross formed by the solstices and the equinoxes symbolises for man the continual battle of the elements both in nature and within his own soul.

While the solstices have to do with the creation and destruction of form as a vehicle of the spirit, the equinoxes have to do with the Christing of the soul, with its development of strength and wisdom through continual struggle with the lower nature. This battle leads eventually to the crucifixion of the lower self and the soul's resurrection to eternity. The supreme example of the Christing of the soul has been given to the western world

in the life and crucifixion of Jesus. In the east, the Bhaga-
vad Gita tells of the warrior Arjuna being guided and
illumined by his charioteer Krishna, who drives him into
the battle. Krishna (Christ) is the Sun, driving the char-
iot of the soul through life's experience and gradually
bringing to it the wisdom which comes from complete
surrender of the human will to the divine—a crucifixion
which leads to resurrection and immortality.

Aries' ruler is Mars, which is closely linked with the
Sun because the Sun is exalted in Aries, a fire sign. Aries
rules the head, the intellect developed to master the problems of physical matter. Mars, the warrior (typified by
Arjuna or by Christian of PILGRIM'S PROGRESS), is the
vehicle of the solar power which works through the mind
and the senses, giving man the will to live, the will to
fight and master the problems of the earth life. His archangel Samael is an angel of fire.

Libra's ruler is Venus, but it is also closely linked with
Saturn, polar opposite of the Sun, for in Libra, a cardinal
sign, Saturn is exalted. The angels of Venus awaken the
soul to the presence of the tester—the Satan (Saturn) of
the lower self which will pull us down to selfishness,
indulgence, spirit sloth, and worldliness; they awaken a
recognition of our duty to others, to act for the good of
the whole. Like Mars, Venus stimulates the mind, but not
only the mind of earth. She awakens our perceptions of
the inner world of light, from which we can receive
strength and inspiration for the battle. The archangel of
Venus is Haniel, whose work is to refine, beautify and
direct the crude outrush of the martian natural energy so
that it will shape matter creatively rather than destructively.
Together Mars and Venus represent the pleasure–pain
principle in life, and in Libra, the scales, we have the
symbol of the point of balance, which the soul must
achieve to find heaven.

The observance of a period of self-discipline through fasting and prayer at Lent (which is now largely ignored except by the devout) is linked with the exaltation of Saturn in Libra, where the full Moon associated with the Spring Equinox is placed. While Saturn represents the dragon of the lower nature, he is also the wise teacher, showing the path of self-discipline which is the only way to gain the spiritual strength to overcome our mortality. Each of the planets has its positive and negative side. Their angels can lift us on wings of light into a consciousness of heaven or can pull us down into misery and self-will.

In the meditations leading up to Easter this great cross of sacrifice of all the elements of the lower self forms the basic theme. Yet the cross of sacrifice is encircled with divine love, bringing deeper understanding of the wondrous plan which is working out in every life. To every soul must come, in a greater or lesser degree according to its karma, a battle which brings turmoil to the emotions, pain to the body, doubt and fear to the mind. In our meditations at the equinoctial full Moons we learn to withdraw from the battle—from all our fears and desires into the stillness and peace of the heart-chakra, where blooms the rose of divine love. If we are suffering through the action of others, let us meditate on the words of Jesus, *Father, forgive them; for they know not what they do.* All souls must eventually suffer crucifixion, and when we turn our thoughts in childlike trust to the Great Healer, who on the cross said, *Father, into thy hands I commend my spirit*, we feel the blessed warmth of love pouring into our hearts. Then the old hard stone of the lower mind is rolled away from the tomb, and we are filled with deep happiness as we realise the presence in us of the arisen Christ—the saviour.

It may seem strange that the feast of St Michael, the angel of the sun, occurs when the Sun is in Libra, the sign of its fall. The associated full Moon is in Aries, the martian sign of battle. Again deep spiritual symbolism is involved. St Michael is usually pictured with sword held aloft in one hand, the scales in the other, and his foot upon the slain dragon. The Moon in Aries inspires the soul to put on the whole armour of light and fight the dragon of worldliness. As we try to rise into the light, St Michael and his angels help us. We never struggle alone, for when we strive to radiate the Christ star these angels of light draw close to protect and inspire us. Thus the full-Moon meditations at the time of the equinoxes can bring to our hearts a richer understanding of the inner conflict which must be waged while the physical life lasts, and understanding also of the strength and power of the arisen Christ within to heal.

## The new moon in Aries

When the new Moon falls in Aries, some time between March 21 and April 20 each year, the angels of the fire element increase their power. They bring a release of divine energy which quickens the soul's enthusiasm, confidence and hope. The Aries new Moon is one of the best times of the year for starting fresh enterprises, for reorganising, for putting plans into practical operation. Remember, however, that this sign comes under Mars, whose angels test humanity by stimulating impulse, desire, self-will and combativeness.

The new Moon can stimulate either the self-will and independence of the limited earth-personality, or the illumined courage of the soul who surrenders all personal desire to the light of the God within. The whole purpose of man's incarnation is that gradually this sun-spirit locked within shall rise triumphant over the little self, to illumine the mind and direct the whole life. This can only happen as the soul learns to transmute the fire of self-will into the clear flame of selfless love.

Perhaps the most helpful meditation at the time of the new Moon in Aries will be on this still flame. Because Aries rules the head and Mars is very much a planet of action, it may not be easy to quieten down the excitements and enthusiasms of the outer self, which could be much caught up with practical interests. It is worth persevering, not so much by trying to clamp down on mental excitements but by focusing the mind on the still flame. Flame is magnetic; it holds the attention so that gradually the soul becomes so absorbed into it that all other thoughts dissolve. You may notice that the fascination makes you feel a little tense at the brow-centre—but consciously relax it, breathing quietly and gently until you feel that your whole being, though alight, is utterly at peace. Your outer mind can become so unobtrusive that you find yourself in the heart of the flame, aware only in your heart-centre. Your whole being radiates warmth and divine love. You feel a sense of self-surrender and worship, of union. If you can hold this vision you will begin to feel the enfolding wings of the great fire angel, the server of the Lord. You will feel the presence of your Master, and the sword of the spirit, of divine truth, in your hand.

As you return to the consciousness of the outer self you will feel the upsurging joy of the angels of the flame filling you with courage and resolution for the service that lies ahead.

## The new moon in Libra

The new Moon in Libra will fall some time between September 23 and October 24 each year. Libra signifies the law of equilibrium, the balancing of the positive and negative lifestreams. An air sign of cardinal or active qua-

lity, it is one of the most subtle influences of the entire
zodiac, for it blends an active mind with gentle and
loving feelings. It is the sign of partnership and mar-
riage—both the physical and spiritual union of man and
woman and, at a much deeper level, the mystical mar-
riage of the soul—with Christ the beloved.

With the Sun and Moon both in Libra when the moon
is new, the angels of the air element quicken the mental
powers and the perceptions; but to touch the hidden
strength and beauty of this influence the soul must
become unusually still and poised. The advanced soul
who has this sign emphasised in his chart can be most
perceptive and intuitive. The exaltation of Saturn in this
sign gives a hint also of the creative power of clear, controlled thought—a power that can only be used when all
the conflicts of the lower mind are stilled; when mind and
feelings are held in a perfect state of balance, such as is
seen in nature when the calm water of a lake appears to
meet and blend with the still sky. The whole countryside
can be so clearly reflected in the waters that it is difficult
to tell where reality ends and reflection begins. When
such a state is achieved in the mind, an image can be
projected into the ether so clearly that it will take form in
the physical world.

At this new moon the angels of Venus, angels of beauty
and love, will more easily draw close to the soul who can
achieve such stillness of mind and body. The perfection of
the heaven-world will be reflected on the still waters of
the soul. Just as the rising and setting sun flood the still
water with glorious light, so can the angels of Venus
bring a heightened awareness of the beauty of the heaven
world, and of union with the Beloved. They quicken our
sense of hearing so that we become aware of celestial harmonies. All the senses of the soul may be quickened.

This divine or celestial consciousness will quicken the

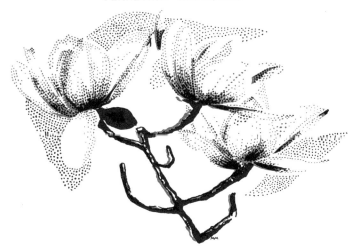

creative faculties of the artist, and the perceptive understanding of those involved in delicate negotiation and
peacemaking, giving them the tact to 'pour oil on troubled
waters'. No matter what their need or occupation, souls
who can attune themselves to the vibrations of this new
moon will be blessed by the angels of Venus.

# 9

## The Moons of the Fixed Cross

### The Taurus–Scorpio Moon Cycle

#### The full moons

The Taurus–Scorpio full moons occur some time between April 20 and May 21 (when the Sun is in Taurus) and between October 24 and November 22 (when the Sun is in Scorpio). Taurus and Scorpio, like Leo and Aquarius, are fixed signs, the signs of stability and emotional depth. People with the fixed signs emphasised in their birth charts are usually steadfast, determined, faithful characters with the will-power to achieve their objectives through steady perseverance over a long period. The fixed signs, above all, give the ability to 'keep on keeping on'.

The houses of the horoscope with which these signs of the fixed cross are connected are all concerned with matters about which people feel deeply: personal possessions, security, children, love affairs, creative power, death, loss, friendship; in the old astrological textbooks, desires, hopes and wishes. Perhaps the deepest lesson which all the fixed signs have to teach the soul is, *Lay up for yourselves treasures in heaven, where neither moth nor rust doth corrupt, and where thieves do not break through nor steal; for where your treasure is, there will your heart be also.*

Taurus especially is much concerned with material possessions, particularly with the physical body and its five senses, through which we receive so much pleasure in

99

beauty and comfort, and so much pain when in deprivation, discomfort or ugliness. Taurus represents not only the physical body, which is the individual temple of the spirit, but the corporate 'body' of all humanity. When men have grown so much in harmony that humanity as a whole forms a living temple of the spirit, the whole substance of the earth will be illumined.

When we speak of the physical body, we mean much more than the bones and flesh and blood of which it is composed. When we think of a person we think not only of the physical body, but the personality as expressed in their mannerisms, desires, opinions and prejudices, and of their clothes and possessions, which so clearly portray their character and outlook. When the spirit leaves the body, what is left is just a shell, utterly different from that vital, living, breathing personality which animated what is now just matter.

At the time of the full Moon when the Sun is in the beautiful Venusian sign of Taurus, the Moon is in Scorpio, the mystical sign of death and regeneration, ruled by Mars, the warrior and the seer. The house of the horoscope which Scorpio rules, the eighth, is often dreaded as the house of death and loss. It is the part of the zodiac which brings to every soul at some time the anguish of bereavement, not only of people we love but of material possessions, of ideas, illusions or opinions which have become dear. All of us in our time worship the golden calf in some form or another. All of us long for some object we think will bring happiness. The further we progress along the spiritual path, the more subtle grows the temptation. We may not worship the cruder aspects of Mammon, money and material position, yet many a graven image do we bow down to instead.

Every time the fear of loss enters our thoughts, we may be sure that we have been concentrating upon a golden calf which has obscured our vision of reality. The signs of Taurus and Scorpio test the ability of the soul to see beyond the fragile illusion of form to the eternal reality. Only when we are free from the illusion can fear be replaced by certainty that our lives are in God's hands, and that in divine love all needs are met. In the words of St Theresa, 'Whom God possesseth, in nothing is wanting. Alone God sufficeth.'

When the heart is empty of personal desire, it is open to the inflow of divine love.

This state of mind cannot be attained by thinking. It is one thing to read books and to know all the theory but quite another to be able to put it into practice. Although we all dread the physical loss of our dear ones, dread enforced change and removal from familiar conditions, it is often these very experiences which bring an understanding of the deep peace and strength of the inner world.

The symbol of Scorpio is still water, the water of the soul, the deeps of eternal life in which all souls have their being. The full Moon is in this sign, in opposition to the Sun in Taurus, at the period of the year which is known in the East as the Wesak festival, the festival of the Lord Buddha, who shows the way to union with the eternal spirit.

To those who are becoming sensitive through meditation, the outpouring of spiritual power at this time from the angels of Venus and Mars and of the Sun and the Moon can bring beautiful enlightenment, but to experience this spiritual beauty, the mind and emotions must become still and the soul like the calm lake reflecting perfectly every detail of the earth and sky. As we surrender the little self, with its fears and resentments, we find ourselves imperceptibly drawn into this state of peace, wherein the Lord Buddha and all the shining souls are gathered together for the festival of worship. The deep peace of the Buddha encompasses us.

In October–November, when the Sun is in the magical sign of Scorpio and the Moon in Taurus, there is a similar thinning of the veil between the two worlds. Often it coincides with the festivals of All Saints, All Souls or Remembrance. In the northern hemisphere there is inevitably sadness, associated with the fall of leaves and the withdrawal of life back into the root. The full Moon in Taurus is in the sign of perfected physical form. It is a temptation to regret the passing of the physical form whether of loved ones or of the Summer's creation in nature. But this is a time to think not of the physical body, but of the dear personality which shone through it, as unchanged as a person is who comes in from outside and removes heavy boots and greatcoat. The person is freer, lighter and more individual, not less. The greatest barrier to our communion with those beyond death is the physical mind which only accepts the impressions of the five senses. As soon as we can quieten the head-mind, the glow of love as we remember those in spirit, opens our heart-minds to communion with them.

Late Autumn is a time of such stillness in nature. If we can respond to it, especially at the time of the Scorpio–Taurus full Moon, we shall find the veil between the two worlds will melt right away, as we learn how to meet heart to heart with those we love in the world of spirit. The heart communion can remove completely any fear of death.

### The new moon in Taurus

The new Moon in Taurus occurs some time between about April 20 and May 21, in the springtime of the year in the northern hemisphere, or in the Autumn in the southern hemisphere, periods of new green life and blossom, or when the trees are clad in their richest colours and every plant bears the seed of regeneration and fresh life. Every sign when in full manifestation in the physical world is also reflecting its polarity in the inner world. At the time of the full moon this polarity is absolutely balanced, the full moon symbolising the perfect form of the soul-temple illumined by the Christ sun, a symbol particularly strong with the sign of Taurus, ruled by the planet of harmony and beauty, and the sign in which the symbol of the soul is exalted.

All the fixed signs have a special significance in the soul-life, for they symbolise the perfect manifestation of their own element. They show how to use the experiences of joy and sorrow, frustration and freedom, creativity and inertia as bricks in the eternal temple of the soul. They are the signs which bring achievement through sustained effort. Tremendous emotional power is locked in these signs, giving them a steadfastness which seems irresistible. When emphasised in a life they bring conditions which seem to be static over such a long period that when change does at last come it can happen rather dramatically. They also cause a condition of mind resistant to the pressure of outside circumstances, and of all the fixed signs perhaps Taurus would seem to be the most fixed, because earth is the heaviest and most static of the four elements. This perhaps is why in THE PATH OF THE SOUL White Eagle states that the earth-initiation is the final one, in which the spirit masters all the physical atoms.

It is perhaps not so easy to respond in meditation to the new moon in Taurus because of the strength of the earth element and the fixed quality. The soul imprisoned in a physical body finds it much easier to respond to comfort, warmth and pleasure than to exercise the necessary spiritual discipline. Yet the beauty of nature should inspire those who would see the power and harmony of the

103

angels of Venus, shining through the earth element at this time.

All physical form has an etheric counterpart closely linked with the earth element, and the inner world at this time can perhaps most easily be contacted by means of the etheric counterpart of the physical senses. If it is possible to sit in a quiet garden, a wood, or some other place of natural beauty, or even just to contemplate a beautiful flower-arrangement, this will help you to respond to the inner world. As you sit relaxed and poised, contemplate the perpetual serenity of the earth element. Let your mind dwell on the quiet hills and downlands, the beauty of the garden or the perfection of a flower.

Because Taurus rules the throat and the voice, a spoken prayer or mantram will help you to become more sensitive, more responsive to the life beyond the physical. Let the higher senses be quickened, especially to the perfume of the flowers, the newly-turned earth, the scent of water, the delicate perfume in the breeze.

As these senses become more aware, you may be able to

visualise very clearly a garden with a still lily pool on which a pure white lotus slowly unfolds. Do not make a great mental effort to do so but rather feel an increasing peace as the spiritual senses respond to the beauty around you. As when meditating on the flame, you will find gradually that the picture of the lotus is forming within the heart. The stiller you are, the more perfect it becomes as the angels of Venus, the angels of beauty, draw close. Rest in this stillness, and if you can hold it devotedly, with quiet will-power, you will feel within your heart, at the heart of the lotus, the shining jewel reflecting in myriad colours the glory of the sun.

As you come back to the earthly consciousness you will be so filled with this radiant inner world that you will long to make a regular habit of meditation. One of the most helpful qualities of Taurus is the ability to form a habit, to establish a ritual which builds power. You will find that your own ritual for meditation, using the same words, at the same time and where possible in the same place every day, will help you to build a bridge between the two worlds which can be of inestimable value in daily life.

## The new moon in Scorpio

Those who live in the country will I am sure agree that at a certain point in the autumn an almost unearthly stillness seems to brood over the whole landscape, as if all life were waiting, expecting a great event. It is like the stillness that one can sometimes feel at the birth of a child. Likewise, when the angel of death draws close there may be the same stillness in the atmosphere.

The fixed sign of Scorpio, whose new Moon occurs between October 24 and November 22, is deeply concerned with these mysteries of life and death. In our clinical world, the brisk routine of the hospital often obscures from us the sacredness of these occasions, and we may miss a great deal. At these moments of birth and death the two worlds meet, and there comes to us all an opportunity to commune, if only momentarily, with those beautiful angelic beings who hold man's destiny in their hands.

This October–November time also brings still conditions in nature which impress us to pause in the busy rush of practical affairs. When both the Sun and Moon are conjoined in the same degree of Scorpio, nature herself provides the conditions for the thinning of the veil between the two worlds. The ghostliness of Halloween is now a source of fun and amusement. But its tales remind us not only that the inner world is real but also that those who seek to discover it should do so wisely. Psychic powers are not to be lightly tampered with. Remember Scorpio is the sign of deep mysterious water, water which can cover bogs and quicksands. Those who earnestly seek to understand the mysteries of life and death must, like Christian in PILGRIM'S PROGRESS, be prepared for a long, hard journey abounding in pitfalls, though the fixed quality of the sign gives its children some of the necessary determination.

Mars, the traditional ruler of Scorpio, is associated with the astral or desire-plane. The lesson which this sign teaches the soul is that peace only comes through surrender of the little self to the great eternal self. The meditation for the Scorpio new Moon, as with the full Moon, is concerned with letting go all desires, be they for material, emotional or mental things. Perhaps the latter are the most subtle of all, the most difficult to recognise and let go; for instance, the desire to shine before others or the desire to gain spiritual advancement. The eastern teachings indicate that one of the simplest paths to peace through self-surrender is that of love and devotion, devotion to a divine personality or to a cause: altruistic work for humanity, or total service to one of the arts and sciences without thought of personal recognition. Souls who have found and recognised their own spiritual teacher, their guru, follow him as their shepherd. Selfless devotion is a quality of all the fixed signs, and before it the relinquishment of the little self becomes as nothing.

At the time of the new Moon in Scorpio, let us lovingly remember our dear ones in the beyond with this truth in mind, consciously letting go any sadness at our own loss and thinking of them as in a glorious sun or star of blazing light; and so rise with them into that world of light. Let us then think with great love of that particular Christed soul with whom we feel especially attuned, whether it is Jesus, Buddha, Krishna, Rama; let us open our whole being to the love which flows from their hearts into ours, a love which is absolute peace and heavenly joy. Through the help of the angels of the sign of Scorpio we can feel, even if only for a brief moment, that deep eternal peace which is untouched by anything that life or death of the body can bring.

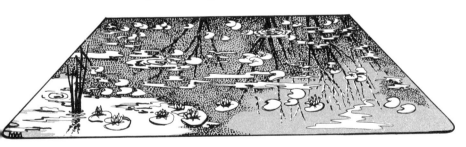

## The Leo–Aquarius Moon Cycle

### The full moons

The full moons which emphasise the signs of Leo and Aquarius occur between January 21 and February 19

(Aquarius) and July 23 and August 23 (Leo) each year. These full moons can greatly stimulate the heart-consciousness, the higher mind, so that if we can attune ourselves to their spiritual radiation we shall become intensely aware of the true meaning of the brotherhood of all life in all God's worlds.

The symbolism of Leo (ruled by the Sun) and Aquarius (ruled first by Saturn, but as man awakens spiritually also closely associated with Uranus) is beautiful, for it emphasises the eternal truth that man is made in the image of God.

Leo, the radiant sun sign symbolised by the lion, king of beasts, portrays the idea that the light, the very essence of eternal life, is set in the heart of the physical body, the body, that animal aspect of man which must first be humanised by the development of thought and reason and then immortalised by the power of the sun, the Christ. With its sensations of pleasure, pain, sorrow, joy, hunger and satiety, the physical body is the training ground in which the spirit of man develops and matures. Ideally the sign of Leo expresses the joy, the creativity and the simple faith of a healthy child.

Aquarius, the man with the watering pot, represents friendship and brotherhood. It is ruled by Saturn, the planet of purity and perfection, discipline and determination. Aquarius indicates the pattern by which man will become perfect. In the northern hemisphere, the period when the Sun is passing through Aquarius often brings snow, and the form of the snowflake is always a perfect six-pointed star pattern. The ancient Jewish symbol of Solomon's seal, the interlaced triangles, signifies the human trinity of body, soul and spirit united with the divine Trinity. This six-pointed star is similar to the eastern symbol for the heart-chakra and both these speak to man's higher consciousness of the in-dwelling spirit,

Christ in the heart of man. White Eagle, whose teachings are intended to lead us towards the inner mysteries of the coming Aquarian Age, gives us the symbol not of the interlaced triangles—which can emphasise the limitation of a purely mental concept of truth—but the outline of the two triangles blended into a shining six-pointed star, the symbol of man made perfect and irradiated by the sun.

As the Aquarian Age advances a particular problem will be the increasing dominance of the lower mind and intellect. Aquarius is an air sign, and air is the most volatile of the four elements. The increasing power of this element in human life has brought about mental stimulation in all aspects of society, accompanied by ever-increasing ease of communication and travel. We are only at the beginning of man's period of exploration of the air element, which will bring unexpected discoveries about the nature of space and man's ability to reach inner and higher spheres of being through thought-power.

At the present time the mental quickening, a veritable explosion of ideas in books, press, radio and television, is almost overwhelming. Such pressure causes overstimulation of the nerves and emotions, resulting in much sickness of nervous origin and the wholesale prescription of tranquillisers, anti-depressants and sleeping drugs.

The restoration of bodies and souls is the work of the true Aquarian, and all who are born with the Leo–Aquarius polarity predominant in their charts could be ministering to other people in some way, especially in work which brings happiness (through entertainment, or developing individual creativity) or in some kind of social service. Group activity is essential to the true Aquarian, who also has a natural instinct for dispassionate friendship. He never tries to possess or dominate but shares the interests and sympathies of a wide variety of companions, at the same time preserving for himself a little circle of independence. Much as the Aquarian loves companionship he also enjoys his times of solitude, preferably in natural surroundings. Since love of natural life is a powerful feature of this temperament, it is possible that as the Aquarian influence gains a stronger hold there will be a wider and more effective effort to restore the peace and beauty of the countryside.

Recognition of the dignity of the human spirit and of the individual's need for the light within is also shown in the natural tolerance of the Leo temperament, which partakes of the qualities of the sun, shining alike on saint and sinner. Leo is the fixed fire sign and its subjects show all the impulsiveness and spontaneity of that element, a basic generosity and giving forth which can even be overwhelming to others unless it is wisely directed. This is where the moderating and disciplining power of Saturn, ruler of Aquarius, can be helpful. People working under the influence of these two signs often do well in partnership because the warm impulsiveness and creativity of Leo is given practical shape and direction by the more realistic Aquarian mind. Leo intuitively recognises and responds to the glory of God and has faith in man's innate divinity. The Aquarian accepts with humour the limitations of human nature. He knows that he who would love his brother man must not expect too much of him. He helps his Leo friend in a practical way, while Leo helps the Aquarian to raise himself beyond the limitations of a sometimes depressed mental state and to unfold his higher consciousness. Both can use the power of thought to help others.

During the few days on either side of these full moons the most helpful meditations will be based on the six-pointed star. In February, when the Sun is in Aquarius and the Moon in Leo, it will probably be most helpful to still the mind by focusing all the attention on the Sun. Sit in the radiance of the spiritual sun and feel its light permeating every atom of body and soul. Gradually the higher consciousness becomes active and we become aware of shining companions, brothers of the light. As the higher consciousness is awakened we feel more and more deeply our unity with the great brotherhood of men and angels, with whom we work for the upliftment and Christing of all humanity. Ever-wider vistas of the beauty and glory of man's future state begin to unfold.

In July, when the Moon is in Aquarius and the Sun in Leo, we may find it easier to make the deep spiritual contact with others in a group, such as in a religious service, or a group meditation. The discipline required in group work, and also the united soul-strength of a group of people all dedicated in service, will attract the angels of light, who will lift the whole gathering beyond the limitations of the lower consciousness into the sun-temple. The true self of the individual will be free for a short time from the limitations of personal desires and opinions, and all are unified in worship of the Christ-being, bathed in the peace and love which radiates from him–her. In childlike simplicity and humility they may be able to touch his seamless robe, radiant with sunlight, and be healed.

### The new moon in Leo

The new Moon in Leo falls some time between July 23 and August 23, high Summer in the northern hemisphere, mid-Winter in the South. When Sun and Moon are conjoined in this radiant fixed fire sign, it is possible for the solar body to be brought into fuller manifestation so that it illumines the whole personality. This was demonstrated by the master Jesus at the Transfiguration, when his solar body shone so brightly that the disciples who were with him were raised in consciousness and became aware of heavenly companions.

Leo rules the heart-chakra, and with the strengthening of the heart-mind through regular meditation the individual solar body gradually takes command of the whole personality and physical instrument. The conjunction of the Sun and Moon in Leo brings to the whole earth a bright and beautiful ray of the Christ Sun. At this time, if we can sufficiently still the clamour of the senses and open the heart-mind to this great ray of light and love we should be filled with joy and thanksgiving, for Leo is a sign of joy.

Leo gives a happy, sunny nature; it is also the sign of children, of love affairs and of pleasurable activities: it fills the soul with vitality and the longing to create physically or artistically. At the same time the joyous appreciation of all the good things in life can lead to self-indulgence and a worldliness which blunts the spiritual perceptions. Yet Saturn is the polar opposite of the Sun and Moon and his powerful discipline is an important factor in constructively channelling the divine energy of the sun. The fiery impulses which spontaneously arise in the human heart need to be directed by the wisdom of Saturn, a truth shown astrologically at the time of this full Moon.

As the soul or psyche is always symbolised by the water element, it is interesting that the eastern symbol for the heart-chakra, the six-pointed star, is also the shape of the snowflake. We have here a demonstration of how the influence of Saturn, planet of contraction and crystallisation, shapes the soul-force into a beautiful six-pointed star which is at the same time irradiated by the Christ sun in the heart.

When the new Moon falls in Leo it is helpful consciously to withdraw both from the pleasures of the senses and even more from the sophistication of the mind. Leo is the sign of childhood. Did not Jesus say, *Except ye be converted, and become as little children, ye shall not enter into the kingdom of heaven?* To respond to the glorious solar power at this time we have to find childlike simplicity and trust. Then the divine love leads us right into the presence of the Great Healer. In purity of adoration for the glorious solar Lord, the Golden One, all weariness vanishes, all sadness, all frustration. The soul becomes transfigured. There is no separation; we are one with the Christ sun. If we can touch this state of of consciousness even for a few moments, the healing power of the Christ will flow through every cell of the body and will flow forth through every thought.

## *The new moon in Aquarius*

The new Moon in Aquarius falls between about January 21 and February 19, and when both Sun and Moon are placed on the same degree of this fixed air sign there is special emphasis on the power of thought. Traditionally Aquarius is ruled by Saturn, the planet of forethought and methodical planning, and in the new age of Aquarius mankind is destined to learn more about the power of thought and the inner soul world of man. Already, in the computer, he has a simple model of the human brain, and is beginning to understand the electrical impulses by which it forms habits of thought. By thought man brings his personal environment under control, and the computer analogy suggests the spirit as programmer of the human brain, and so of the creative power of thought. Leo, the polar opposite of Aquarius, rules the heart centre; it is the great sign of creativity. White Eagle tells us that with spiritual unfoldment we shall learn how to bring into operation the mind in the heart. The head-mind, which has to be so active in everyday affairs, can produce foolish 'programmes' which destroy more than they create, and thought-habits which produce tension, anxiety and disease.

As the Aquarian Age gains a stronger hold on the thought-life of humanity we shall notice a great increase in future planning, as men recognise that all nations

are so closely linked that by chain reaction happenings in one part of the world affect people everywhere. We are moving steadily towards the time when the suffering of one will be the suffering of all and the brotherhood of nations will have to become a reality.

The period of the new Moon in Aquarius is a specially powerful time for radiating the Christ-light into the heart of humanity. This light will quicken in all people the urge towards brotherhood and kindly understanding of each other's needs.

To bring the heart-mind into conscious operation, it is essential to spend some time every day in quiet contemplation, and so gradually become more aware of the power and glory of God, which dwells deep within every human being. It is interesting that Saturn rules both the signs through which the Sun passes at the beginning of the year when many people make some attempt at self-assessment and start planning for the year ahead. With the Sun and Moon both in Aquarius, the angels of Saturn are especially active and we can call upon their help in this task.

In chapter two we described a method for 'programming' the subconscious mind, just before dropping off to sleep, and if possible on first waking. This can be a powerful help in creating a mental state which will improve physical health, and now is a good time to check and if necessary reset our programme. In this way we can gradually build into the soul the positive qualities we know are needed and eliminate the less desirable ones.

Since the symbol of the heart-chakra is also the symbol for the Aquarian Age and of man made perfect, it is right that our meditation at this time should concentrate on the six-pointed star. Let us first go in imagination into the quiet hills. *I will lift up mine eyes unto the hills, from whence cometh my help*, sings the Psalmist. In the stillness we look towards the rising sun, and in the heart of it visualise the form of the six-pointed star, shining white and radiant. Let us hold this thought as steadily as possible, not in the mind, but in the heart. At first we shall consciously have to direct the mind, but with steady breathing and quiet concentration, the control-centre will imperceptibly change from the head to the heart. Let us just be still and know God, radiating through our whole being from this star in the heart.

In this star-consciousness we are functioning in our

own body of light, and can unite with others to radiate light and healing, both to individuals and to conditions in the world. Let us think clearly of anyone in need and see them right in the heart of the star. Hold the thought for a few seconds, and then in the name of Christ—the sun in our hearts and the universal sun in the heart of humanity—call upon the angels to continue the healing which we have initiated.

When there is political strife, or industrial unrest, instead of feeling helpless we can use this method to bring wisdom to those in a position of responsibility, never taking sides, but just radiating divine light to the whole situation.

# 10

# *The Moons of the Mutable Cross*

## *The Gemini–Sagittarius Moon Cycle*

### *The full moons*

The Gemini–Sagittarius full Moons occur some time between May 21 and June 22 (Sun in Gemini) and between November 22 and December 22 (Sun in Sagittarius). These full moons have a special significance in that they lead the way into the solstices, those great turning-points of the year which also symbolise the turning-points in the evolution of the soul: its descent into matter, and its awakening to the light with the birth of the Christ.

The full moon in Gemini is known as the Christ moon, one of the most powerful periods in the whole year. Its symbolism is linked with the Christian festival of Whitsun, which celebrates the anointing of the twelve disciples with the power of the Holy Spirit.

In the story told in the Acts of the Apostles the disciples, who were all feeling keenly the physical loss of their beloved master and teacher, had withdrawn to an upper room. This can be interpreted in the ordinary physical sense and in the sense that all of them had in prayer and meditation withdrawn to the upper or inner chamber of their own being. *And when the day of Pentecost was fully come, they were all with one accord in one place.* They were of one mind, in harmony with each other, their hearts and minds focused on communion with the Christ.

Perhaps only those who have experienced the at-one-ment which can come in group meditation, in which all

117

the members are perfectly attuned one with another, comprehend the wonder of those disciples as their heavenly consciousness was awakened by the divine fire. When the Sun is in Gemini and the Moon at the full in the fire sign of Sagittarius, ruled by Jupiter, the planet governing the celestial body, there can come a most beautiful outpouring of spiritual power upon souls who withdraw into their inner sanctuary and aspire to the heaven-world, quickening their consciousness to knowledge of the cosmos.

Gemini and Sagittarius are mutable signs, which means that they combine the will to action of the cardinal cross with the stability of the fixed cross. In a sense the mutable signs represent the wisdom-aspect of the Trinity, in which opposites always become reconciled. This truth is symbolised in the Caduceus of Mercury. In the legend, at its touch two quarrelling snakes immediately twined themselves round the wand in complete harmony. This story is of course deeply symbolic of the positive–negative lifestreams which, when perfectly balanced, produce light; or on the inner planes raise the soul into a new dimension of consciousness.

The trials and conflicts of the mutable cross are fought out in the mind far more than in the physical life, and people who have many planets in mutable signs, except perhaps when Virgo is emphasised, tend to find the world of thought more real than the physical. Mental pressures and conflicts bring disturbance to their nervous system, which is usually highly-strung and tense, causing irritability and nervous exhaustion. Nevertheless Mercury and Jupiter govern all the communication systems of mind, soul and body, and it is under their power that the heavenly messengers, angels of light, can draw close to bless and protect the soul, or alternatively the angels of darkness whisper their destructive messages into the unsuspecting ear until the soul is pulled down into darkness and negativism.

The gift of the angels of Mercury and Jupiter to man is a growing awareness of the powers both of light and darkness, and of man's ability, through controlled thought and breathing, to balance and govern these two aspects of life. The great archangel of Mercury is known as Raphael, and that of Jupiter, Zadkiel. All the archangels of the planets have hosts of lesser beings working under their direction, many of whom are drawn to human beings as guardian angels to watch over their destiny. The magic of the full Moons is generated by the power of these angels, which explains why our meditations at these times can prove specially helpful and illuminating if we can attune ourselves with the particular planetary power.

The full moon in Gemini, the Christ moon, in a sense prepares the soul to respond to the outpouring of the Christ-radiance at the solstice. With the Sun in the airy Gemini and the Moon in the fiery Sagittarius the conditions in the soul-world are especially helpful for the reception of heavenly inspiration and an awakening of the higher consciousness. One might liken this full Moon to the time when Jacob in great tribulation laid his head upon a stony pillow and had the vision of the ladder going right into heaven with angels, beautiful winged beings, passing up and down, bringing their blessing from heaven to earth.

At the time of the Christ moon in May–June and the Advent moon in November–December, there is always a stimulation of the mind, which is felt more keenly by people with the mutable signs emphasised in their birth-charts. This stimulation makes it more difficult to control the nervous system and a real effort must be made to hold the balance between the positive and negative thoughts. The practice of God-breathing, in which we consciously draw in the divine breath and feel its peace and tranquillity pervading the whole being, will be especially helpful. If we quietly persist, with every breath becoming more still and relaxed, and the mind held like a clear mirror reflecting the sun, we may feel ourselves raised to the portals of the universal temple of wisdom. It can only be approached through the sun. In the heart of this radiant sun we become aware of the two pillars at the entrance, one black, one white, perfectly balanced; they now appear each as a great angelic being, one in a cloak of light, one in a cloak of darkness. Between the pillars we gaze into a

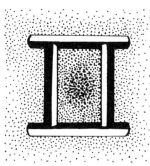

light indescribable in earthly terms. We feel the rush of the divine fire of love, a flame leaping through heart and mind, filling us with compassion, forgiveness, and full understanding as we pass through the portals of the great temple into the Christ-presence. This experience of union brings to the soul a glimpse of the true meaning of brotherhood, which involves complete understanding, acceptance of the duality which is present in every soul. It brings forgiveness.

At the time of the Advent moon the Sun is in Sagittarius and the Moon in Gemini. Again there comes the quickening and the strain on the nervous system, especially in those who are sensitive to the conditions in the soul-world. Again there is the emphasis on the preparation of the outer consciousness so that the soul can be receptive to the special Christmas blessing at the solstice.

At the Advent full moon the Sun in Sagittarius indicates an outpouring of boundless love and compassion upon the soul-life of humanity. The angels of Jupiter draw close in love and wisdom in preparation for the rebirth, in form, of the light, the Christ-babe. The Moon in Gemini can help us to attune mind and nervous system to this blessing of the heavens and the angels of Mercury help to bring it right through into our limited everyday consciousness. Both Jupiter and Mercury are planets of joy, and so the Christmas spirit is expressed in songs and carols, fun and games of all kinds. Also typical of their influence is the exchange of Christmas cards and greetings right across the world as the sun-festival of the winter solstice is ushered in.

### The new moon in Gemini

The new Moon in Gemini (between May 21 and June 21) and the concentration both of solar and lunar power in this mutable air sign bring opportunity for man to quicken his awareness of God, the creator of all life.

All the air signs help to create and expand the mental consciousness. Without this vital faculty man could in no way understand and appreciate the beauty of life and the wonders of creation. The mind is ultimately the creator of the temple of the soul, but before man realises its spiritual potential he passes through a long period of training which teaches him the power of the subconscious and superconscious mind, and leads him to discover that by the power of his intellect he can manipulate matter to an almost unlimited extent.

The Sun in Gemini is perhaps more than any of the other signs symbolic of the gateway into heaven. Its very symbol, the two pillars, black and white, recalls wisdom and indicates the ability of mind to comprehend the positive–negative symmetry of creation, and to marry the opposing elements.

While the Sun and Moon are both in this volatile sign so much spiritual power is shed upon earth that those who can attune themselves to it may be given great illumination. On the other hand the vibrations of this influence are so fine and so stimulating to the nervous system that it is only too easy for the spiritual power to be dissipated in excitement, chatter and disorganised activity. Souls with Gemini strongly emphasised in their charts know only too well how quickly they can be diverted from their object and how difficult it is to concentrate. Yet to realise one iota of the spiritual power in this influence it is essential that mind and body relax and become still.

As we said in connection with the Wednesday meditation Mercury, with Gemini, is specially concerned with the breath, and this state of mental quiet can be attained through gentle, controlled breathing. If you regularly perform the breathing exercises, they grow easier with practice and the knack comes. Listening to the breathing is helpful. Gradually the mind becomes relaxed, like a still pool or a mirror reflecting the sun. If you can maintain this state of stillness there will come an easy transference from the head- to the heart-consciousness, where the radiance of the reflected sun burns as a flame. Relax further and this living light begins to take form. Just as the facets of a diamond reflect countless rays of light and colour so the little personality, being absorbed into the greater self, discovers it can draw upon countless facets of knowledge and wisdom gained through lives in the past and may recognise facets still dull and unpolished, still requiring the grind of physical experience to polish them until they too clearly reflect the divine glory.

In this way the quickened intelligence, which is the gift of the angels of Mercury, brings the soul nearer to a comprehension of the infinite wonder and glory of the Creator. The angels of Mercury are messengers from heaven and those on the mercurial ray may, at times when Mercury is emphasised in the heavens, be enabled to convey to their companions something of the beauty which the soul can win. Truly the angels of Mercury can lend the soul wings with which to free itself from all limitation, yet the very first requisite is perhaps the most difficult: to make the busy outer mind absolutely still.

## The new moon in Sagittarius

The new Moon in Sagittarius (between November 22 and December 22), and the combination of both Sun and Moon in this mutable fire sign, can bring increased responsiveness to inspiration from the celestial plane of being. Jupiter and Sagittarius are concerned with the higher mind, with man's aspiration to the heavens. Jupiter, the law-giver, brings an expansion of the consciousness so that it is able to receive a vision of the outworking of divine law. On the outer plane people coming under Jupiter's influence can be wise judges and professional advisers, and on the spiritual plane his lofty influence can bring still greater blessing. The angels of Jupiter, by their warmth and beneficence, help the little mortal mind to become free of its prejudices and barriers. A man who has travelled widely and made friends with people of all nationalities and all parts of society is more able to take a broad view of life and to know the important from the unimportant than one who has no experience of life beyond his immediate environment. The power of Jupiter especially helps to break down the barrier between the two worlds. When Sagittarius is emphasised in a birth-chart, moreover, the soul may be possessed of an intuitive prophetic quality. He or she will experience hunches, pictures of coming events, possibly through prophetic dreams.

The symbol of Sagittarius is the archer, and the Sagittarian mind works with the swiftness of an arrow going straight to the mark. This fire sign awakens in the heart longing for divine truth and the desire to comprehend with the earthly mind the secrets of the cosmos, which can only be known through the soul rising into a different dimension.

When Sun and Moon are conjoined in Sagittarius there comes a thinning of the veil between the worlds. The wise men discover the star which will lead them to the birthplace of the Christ.

Sagittarius is the sign of travel, both mental and physical; it also rules universities and all places of higher education. It signifies the trained mind of earth which is needed to appreciate the wonder of creation. It also signifies the trained and perfected body, the swiftness of limb, the strength, the clear sight of the athlete. Fiery impulsiveness is both the strength and the weakness of this sign. It is quick on the mark, quick to perceive truth, quick to perceive faults and imperfections, and like all fire signs prone to hasty action.

At the time of the new moon, the most helpful symbol for meditation will most likely be the still, clear, controlled flame reaching heavenward, as if aspiring to touch a most brilliant star. While responding to the impulse of the fire signs, we must remain peacefully relaxed, our whole being concentrated upon purifying and guiding the flame, yet allowing it to grow like a great pillar of light and strength shining through body, heart and mind until that pillar of light seems to constitute the whole being. The beautiful star which was shining above it seems to become more brilliant. The flame rises till it becomes part of the star. The little self is absorbed into the greater self; *I and my Father are one.* From the heart, both of the star and of our being, a tremendous radiation of light and energy pours forth. This is that immense ray of light and love which is being poured upon humanity, preparing their souls for the Christmas blessing. Song, colour, free giving of the self and worship of the Creator express this exultation of the spirit. This is the true preparation for the blessing of Christmas.

## The Virgo–Pisces Moon Cycle

### The full moons

The Virgo full moon occurs some time between August 23 and September 22 and that of Pisces between February 19 and March 21 each year. Like those of the other mutable signs, Gemini and Sagittarius, these full moons lead the way into the seasonal turning points—this time of the equinoxes.

These full Moons, at the end of Winter and Summer in both hemispheres, bring a season to completion. The harvest is gathered in and nothing can increase it or decrease it now. This store of food, traditionally, must see us right through the Winter. By the Spring full moon, Winter is ending and the ground should have been cleared, fertilised and prepared for the seed-planting and the new season's growth. Because of their close association with seed-time and harvest, Virgo and Pisces are especially symbolic of the karma we bring back each time we return to the earth-life—each time the seed of our soul-life is replanted into physical matter. The quality of the seed, the characteristics inherent in the seed, are the result of past seasons' growth and experience. There is nothing we can do about the basic events in our life and the experiences which have to be gone through. The nature of the body we have to use, the physical tendencies to health, disability or sickness, are all brought back in this seed created from a past incarnation. Our opportunity lies in the way we handle our present karma and the efforts we make to sow good seed for the future.

All the signs of the mutable cross are dual in their nature, even Virgo, although her duality is less apparent than that of Gemini, Mercury's other sign. The duality of Virgo lies in the subtle blending of the physical and the etheric world. People with this sign emphasised are often much more psychic, more aware of the etheric plane of the nature kingdom than they realise. The etheric body itself is dual, the lower part so closely interpenetrating the physical and so nearly solid that it can almost be seen with physical sight. This lower etheric body may sometimes be seen as a ghost, when for some reason a soul is earthbound and the lower counterpart has not yet been re-absorbed into the elements. The body of light, the higher etheric, is of much finer substance. It continues after the death of the physical body and in time becomes completely illumined by the solar consciousness.

All matters connected with health, healing, diet, herbs and drugs come under the rulership of Virgo, while Pisces, her polar opposite, is above all the sign of the Great Healer, the sign of the eternal ocean of life, the universal consciousness. When the Moon is full in the sign of Pisces there is a subtle influence of divine peace and wisdom. Being of mutable quality both Virgo and Pisces are wisdom signs. The vibrations at this time are gentle and subtle and the mind and heart must be at peace to receive them. Once again we must remark how quickly the mind will become calm if the breathing is gently slowed down and we turn our thoughts to the still, shining six-pointed star, symbolic of the perfect balance between the earthly and the heavenly consciousness. As we relax in mind and body we begin to feel the peace of a still, shining lake; its waters are so unruffled that it mirrors exactly the surrounding hills.

> Let the boat of the mind glide slowly
> from its moorings
> (Leave the turbulent, restless river)
> Past the soft green fingers of the rushes,
> Into the lake's cool silver,
> Quiet rippling at the prow.*

As we move peacefully towards the still centre of the lake we feel the strength of the surrounding hills, between which the rising sun makes a path of light on the water, which is slightly ruffled by the movement of the boat. The colours of the dawn sky are reflected in the water, making the surface of the lake like a shining rainbow. We feel impelled to bathe in these pools of colour, and find the water gently buoyant—life-giving and refreshing. All strain and weariness is washed away. Now we feel ourselves being drawn along the path of light towards the golden sun. Angel companions lead us into the heart of the sun-temple—into the shining presence of the Great Healer. All care and tension has left us and as simple children we respond to his all-enfolding love and wisdom. Our hearts quicken with love and the desire to serve all creatures of the Lord of life. Herein lies that purity of heart and of motive which enables the soul to see God.

With the Sun in Pisces and the full Moon in Virgo at the end of Winter there is exactly the same need for stillness of mind and body if one is to touch the magic and mystery of the season. The Sun in Pisces quickens the desire of the soul for at-one-ment, while the Moon, in a

* From the poem 'The Lake of Peace', by T. D. See Grace Cooke, *Meditation*, p. 87.

practical earth sign, may well make one feel that the everyday concerns of physical life—health, duty, work— are more important. When earth signs are prominent, making the spiritual contact can be facilitated by harmonious ritual, for this helps to create an etheric bridge between the two worlds. Jupiter, ruler of Pisces, is the planet of ritual, and is closely linked with the seventh ray, the ray of magic. Those who are able to take part in some form of religious ritual, such as a service of communion, may well find themselves able briefly to reach another dimension of consciousness—to be raised into the presence of the Great Healer. One has to start by imagining this beautiful communion—try to picture the pearly whiteness of his robe, his beautiful healing hands, the sunlit warmth and peace of his presence, and the flavour of the bread and the wine—and almost imperceptibly it all becomes real. Deep in our hearts we know that the lord of life has blessed us. His angels continue to enfold us in wings of peace long after the vision has faded.

## The new moon in Virgo

The new Moon in Virgo falls between August 23 and September 23. As Virgo, an earth sign of mutable quality, brings wisdom to the soul, and Mercury, her ruler, is closely associated with the etheric body and the nervous system, and since both are linked with the sixth house in the birth-chart (the house of health and service), the mystery hidden by this sign is of how the mind can be trained to become the server of the spirit, and under its direction bring the physical body to perfection.

The ancient Indian philosophy of yoga clearly demonstrates the power the trained mind can have over the body, and shows the student how to discipline and purify body and mind so that both become more responsive to the guidance of the spirit. Healthy vitalising diet, exercises which strengthen and stimulate the nervous system and ductless glands, together with regular periods of meditation and relaxation, all form part of the yoga training. This all seems closely allied to the principles of discrimination, purity, wisdom and perfection which are the keynotes of the earthy Virgo—sensitive and subtle, yet practical.

The Sun and Moon conjoined in this sign have the effect of loosening the etheric body to make the soul more than usually responsive to the inner worlds and to the

power of spiritual healing. All the earth signs give a feeling for ritual, which is really a means of bringing order and harmony into practical affairs. As at the full moon, religious ritual can be specially helpful in discovering the subtle and beautiful power of the angels of Mercury, and can help to focus the mind upon beauty and raise it above the imprisoning body of flesh.

Virgo, the virgin, symbolises the childlike state of mind, obedient and trusting, accepting with gentle humility the work and experience which life and karma bring. *Behold the handmaid of the Lord; be it unto me according to thy word.*

In the body this sign rules the digestive tract, which absorbs the nourishment from food; in the soul it signifies the ability to absorb the lessons of karma and so partake of the bread of life.

The pure white rose is a beautiful symbol for meditation during this period. Make the mind still and relaxed with the gentle deep-breathing ritual; imagine that with each breath you are drawing into you the pure white light of the brilliant six-pointed star which shines above you.

As you think upon this star, you may gradually become aware of the fragrance of a pure white rose. Try not to force your thoughts with the mind, but feel it in your heart. Feel that this pure and perfect white rose is gently unfolding its petals. You are part of it; your soul is unfolding to the light as the petals of the rose unfold in the sun; you are aware of a heavenly peace pervading your whole being as all earthly thoughts and anxieties drop away and your mind and heart are focused on the rose. See now its golden heart open in the sun. Right in the centre, like a diamond, there is a single dewdrop. Watch the dewdrop sparkling with light and colour. It grows brighter and larger till it seems almost like the sun itself, and in the centre is the beloved form of your own master and teacher. In his tranquil mind you can be still and know God.

The use of affirmations, as described in chapter two, can be specially powerful at this time. Think clearly and carefully of the quality of character or the health conditions which you want to improve and make the affirmation many times as you are dropping asleep. This is a magical secret for building into the subconscious mind positive thoughts of harmony and well-being which after a time manifest in the outer life.

## *The new moon in Pisces*

The new Moon in Pisces falls between February 19 and March 20. Pisces is perhaps the most subtle, gentle and volatile sign of the whole zodiac. It is associated with the twelfth house of the horoscope, the house of secrets, and of confinement from the world. People with this sign strongly emphasised often find themselves drawn to work which involves them in the life of a large establishment such as a hospital, a prison, even a large school: places of social service in which the server almost loses his or her identity in the group-soul of the establishment. There may be conscious dedication to this service, or for some karmic reason the soul may be drawn into it and be in a constant state of conflict and frustration at the personal limitations imposed. This is a sign also of the secret brotherhoods, wherein each member becomes totally dedicated to the work of that particular group. All men at some time undertake such soul-training on the spiritual path towards conscious at-one-ment with the divine life.

Because both Pisces and Virgo are so linked with the seed-time–harvest finality, they symbolise the limitations of our lot. They also symbolise the heavenly help which is always available to the soul striving to serve to the best of his ability, and accepting humbly his own limitations.

The mutable quality and water element quicken the sympathies and draw the soul into close contact with others by psychic awareness of their feelings. Souls under this sign are sometimes functioning more at a psychic than a physical level, which makes them appear to be vague, dreamy and other-worldly. They quickly absorb the moods and impressions of their companions, and this can make life difficult for them unless they have attained a degree of inner strength and awareness of their true self. As they begin to realise why they feel as they do, and what is the purpose of their incarnation, more than the subjects of any other sign they can become attuned to the cosmic rhythms and respond to the help of the angels.

Since Pisces symbolises the sea of cosmic consciousness, perhaps the most helpful picture for meditation will be the sea. Contemplate the wide horizon of the ocean; listen to the sound of the sea birds, the music of the waves and the wind. Feel the rhythm of the tides; see the rising sun shining across the still water, and the great white wings of the angels of wisdom coming forth from the heart of the sun; see them drawing the soul right into the temple—into the presence of the Comforter. The angels of Jupiter will help the soul to rise into a different dimension of consciousness; help him to understand the great teachers when they tell us that the kingdom of heaven lies within. A beautiful religious service, or listening to uplifting music, will help to raise the soul into a higher dimension, and release it from the imprisonment of the physical mind and body.

# 11

# *The Planets and the Planes of Consciousness in Meditation*

In every incarnation we are born into a body with an earthly mentality represented by the first house, which is linked with the sign Aries and the planet Mars. The old symbol for Mars is the cross of matter above the circle of spirit—divine energy taking form in matter. The energy of Mars draws the soul into physical incarnation and manifests through the desire nature giving us the will to live, to achieve, to create and procreate. All this forms the consciousness, the ordinary, everyday mind bounded by time, space and desire. In this book we have been illustrating the way to rise above the limitations of this consciousness and bring perfect balance between the 'outer' and 'inner' consciousness.

In the diagram of the houses of the horoscope, the six-pointed star replaces the circle usually placed in the middle, and symbolises the Christ in man, the light shining in matter, the light which each of us has in our heart and which we have to learn to bring fully into the outer consciousness. The planets and signs represent the different levels of consciousness at which man will eventually learn to function, also the tests and trials which he will meet and overcome on the way—just as do heroes in fairy stories and myths the world over.

The circle of the heavens is reproduced in the soul of each one of us; we live within the circle of our own solar system. Old drawings in the books of the medieval alchemists picture the Grand Man of the Heavens, or the Christ-man, and the little man—the macrocosm and the microcosm. Astrology starts to link with meditation, because the eventual way to cope with the problems of the outer life, with the stresses and cross-vibrations shown in the birth-chart, is for the little man—the soul in incarna-

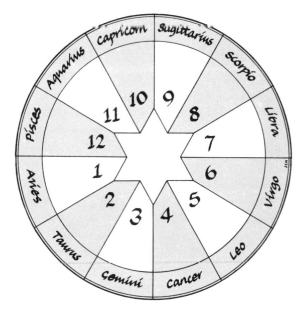

tion—to become consciously united with the Grand Man of the Heavens—the Christ.

The heart of man corresponds to the sun, and the light within him, his spiritual heart, vibrates in harmony with the heart of the universe. In meditation, the first thing that we have to do is to disengage ourselves from the chatter of the outer mind and seek the centre, the sun of our life. We seek to balance the outer and the inner worlds of being; we seek to cross the bridge into that inner world in full consciousness. This balancing of the two states of awareness can be symbolised by Libra, the polar opposite of Aries. The outer mind is essential for dealing with the practical things of life. But if we only live in that mind, we miss the purpose for which the shining spirit has been born into this body of flesh. The whole purpose of incarnation is that the light within, the sun, shall illumine the lower mind and being. As White Eagle puts it, the light of the heart shall irradiate the mind.

Venus, ruler of Libra, is the planet of harmony and beauty. Her symbol, with the circle of the spiritual consciousness, the sun-consciousness, placed above the cross of matter, indicates what we are trying to achieve in meditation.

It is much easier to leave the outer world and go within when there is beauty and harmony around us, so when we meditate we need to find a quiet and harmonious place—it is essential to be able to shut out the bustle of the outside world—which is why early morning and late evening are good times. In the East, sunrise and sunset have always been the chosen times for meditation. These correspond with the Aries–Libra periods of the day. On waking, we are still close to the inner world to which we retired during sleep; in the evening we are preparing to return. The prelude to meditation must be a balancing of the two worlds, and so we become quiet and still—the stillness of the sun rising over the hilltops, flooding the world with light; the peace of sunset, relaxation, letting go the outer world. To help us to find this balance, we close the eyes. When the physical eye is closed, the inner eye, the inner vision, opens. Aries is a fire sign and the element fire governs sight; but the balancing sign, Libra, is an air sign and so is connected with breathing. As we have previously shown, one of the best ways to quieten the outer mind is through controlled breathing. Quiet, even, rhythmic and slightly deeper breathing helps to bring a state of tranquillity.

As the physical senses begin to be closed and the nervous system becomes more relaxed through the gentler, slower breathing, we automatically become more aware of the etheric world, the inner world of nature which interpenetrates physical matter. The etheric plane is closely linked with the earth element, and as we become more conscious of the inner world, we proceed from the Aries Libra plane (first and seventh houses in the diagram) to the Taurus–Scorpio plane (second and eighth).

Taurus, the other venusian sign, is of the earth element, and so is associated with the sense of smell. This sense, aroused by a beautiful fragrance, can help us to become aware of the etheric world. Quite often, the first sign of the presence of someone from the higher world comes through the sense of smell—a little whiff of incense perhaps, or the scent of flowers which we know has no physical source. This is why certain incenses are often used by yogis and in some Christian rituals. One of the first principles of Taurus is obedience, and when we are learning to enter these inner worlds, we are taught that there are certain rules which must be obeyed. We learn how to sit, how to hold the physical body in a comfortable position, with the spine straight and the head poised. We learn that it is important for the physical body to be so relaxed and comfortable that we can forget all about it, but at the same time controlled. Venus, as the planet of beauty and harmony, illustrates the need for peaceful, harmonious physical conditions when we seek to explore the inner worlds. If possible it is good to create your own little sanctuary, even if this is only a corner of your room where you can hang a picture which you find inspiring, and perhaps have some flowers to create a focal point of beauty. Music also helps to release the soul from the thraldom of matter, and it often helps to have certain records or cassettes of quiet music which are kept to play for meditation.

Taurus rules the throat, and at the outset of deep meditation the throat-centre is brought into operation by the chanting of certain words and sounds, the effect of which is to loosen the denser particles of the etheric body and to release the soul from the frontal mind. The hymns and chants of the Christian church have a similar effect to the mantramistic chants of the eastern religions, that of helping the soul become aware of the Word. In the gospel of St John, *In the beginning was the Word . . . and the Word was God.* As you chant, you become conscious of the light within the heart-centre. Your being is concentrated on the light.

The polar opposite of the earthy Taurus is Scorpio, which is connected with the eighth house, the house of death and the inner worlds. In meditation we learn to enter those worlds in full consciousness. As soon as we withdraw from the physical consciousness to enter the inner planes, we shall contact powerful psychic forces of which as yet we know very little. This is why all true spiritual schools teach you that when you enter onto the spiritual path, when you start deep meditation, you should do so under the guidance of a reliable teacher, and be prepared to obey that teacher implicitly. (Remember Taurus is the sign of obedience.) Also it is important to keep to your chosen teacher and not to try to follow several at the same time, which could lead to dangerous confusion.

Scorpio is the sign of fixed water, still water. Having established the contact with the inner light, we then begin to create in imagination our own inner world. Let us imagine that in spirit we are entering a beautiful garden in which is a clear pool, or a lake with still water reflecting the sky. Floating on the water is a closed lily bud. We wait and watch in absolute quiet until it begins to unfold its petals. The still water and the lotus both symbolise the soul, and indicate that only when the soul can achieve this state of absolute stillness and calm can real meditation begin.

This state of controlled stillness is quite different from the blank mental state which some people confuse with meditation, and which can be extremely dangerous since it invites unpleasant psychic intrusion.

Of course, the physical life being what it is, we have to cope with such difficulties as a distracting noise outside, or some little physical discomfort, but gradually, by the will of the spirit, we can learn to overcome these problems. The importance of regular practice in meditation cannot be over-emphasised. Taurus and Scorpio are fixed signs which give determination and will-power, and it is certainly the will to make a habit of it—to 'keep on keeping on' as White Eagle says, which brings success. Gradually we learn how to go deep within the temple of our being, till we feel that we are encircled by a wall of light; our consciousness is so fixed upon the inner light that we just forget all outside disturbances—they cease to exist. We have entered 'the temple of the great silence', in which we can find that strength and refreshment of spirit which we so badly need. It is interesting that the Moon, which symbolises the soul, is exalted in Taurus, sign of the builder.

Now this Taurus–Scorpio stage, when we train ourselves to become absolutely still and steadfastly to seek the inner light until all earthly concerns fall away, is the important preliminary to deep meditation. We are now beginning to function in the higher etheric body, the body of light in which we will gradually become fully aware of the inner world.

Next we come to the mental planes and the two signs of the mind, Gemini and its polar opposite Sagittarius,

138

the third and ninth houses. Gemini, the air sign ruled by the planet Mercury, governs that part of the mind which enables us to think and reason—to interpret the flashes of light and inspiration which come to us from the higher consciousness, governed by Jupiter, lord of the fiery Sagittarius. The higher mind dwells forever in the inner world and can only be brought into operation in prayer and aspiration.

Having become utterly still and, as it were, dead (Scorpio) to the outer world, we are then taught to use our powers of creative imagination. We may be told to visualise a beautiful temple. The two pillars at the entrance of this temple of the spirit are like the symbol of the sign of Gemini. Gemini is a dual sign, and so is its opposite, Sagittarius. As we come to the plane of the mind, the expressive part of man, the creative thinking part, there is always duality, always the question whether our experience is real. With the will of the spirit disciplining the mind we can create so much—we visualise the garden, we visualise the pool. We imagine it, we watch the lotus unfold. We create the pillars of our temple; but at a certain point, and we can never tell when it is going to be, we find that instead of having to create, the picture begins to unfold spontaneously. This halfway house can be very confusing for meditators, as the outer mind questions, 'Is it right, or am I just imagining it?' Sometimes this stage goes on for quite a long time—it may almost be likened to wandering in the wilderness.

You will know without doubt when you have made a true spiritual contact, but it is when you are nearly there that doubt creeps in. When you have built your temple it seems real, but you still need the divine help which comes from your higher self, your Christ-self, to—as it were—bring it alive. This true contact, which comes in a flash of inspiration (Sagittarius), is like a ray of light which brings to the heart such a feeling of joy that it may even cause the tears to flow.

On the other hand, in trying to assess whether a meditation is 'imagination' or the real thing, we need to be somewhat suspicious if we are constantly given pats on the back, crowns or honours of any kind. We could well be indulging in what White Eagle calls 'nebulous glorification'. When we make a real contact with the inner light, we will be filled with such a sense of worship and devotion to the source, to God, that the little self will be forgotten. With the simplicity of a child we feel welling up in our hearts warm divine love which reaches out to all creation.

This brings us within the circle of the heavenly temple, our own soul-temple and the temple of the universe. Let us focus our attention on the star whose light is pouring down upon us.

In this circular temple, with the light shining down from the central dome, we have the symbol of the dot within the circle: that most ancient symbol of the sun which has been inscribed on ancient stones and monuments the world over. The temple built under White Eagle's direction on New Lands hill embodies this symbol: it is a circular temple with the symbols of the signs of the zodiac all round the edge of the dome and the shining star at the centre. These symbols represent all the different types of life on earth in man and bird and beast, in plant and mineral life. All are infused by the light of the sun–star, and through this light are part of the eternal brotherhood of the heaven. As we grow practised in meditation and learn how to enter the temple of our own being, we can contact, through the higher mind, the angelic kingdom: the angels of the elements, the angels of healing, of music, of creative work.

Having made the soul-effort necessary to reach and

enter the heavenly temple, we come to the Cancer–Capricorn, or the Leo–Aquarius stage (fourth–tenth and fifth–eleventh house-pairs). These two pairs can be linked together. Cancer, ruled by the Moon, is the sign of the Divine Mother: Mary; Isis of the Egyptians; the Great Goddess of the Hindus. She creates and rules the temple of

the soul. She represents all the negative signs of the zodiac, the earth and the water signs, the receptive signs—the signs of mother nature, mother earth. Correspondingly Leo, ruled by the Sun, represents the divine

Father, the positive, aspiring, creative, free, fiery spirit that manifests in the fire and air signs.

Those who meditate regularly will find that on certain days, when they enter the temple they feel as if they are going up and up into the heart of the sun. All is light and glory, heavenly sound and colour. The light is dazzling. Yet on other days they are conscious only of a quiet enfoldment, as of a garden or the heart of a rose. This will obviously be a predominantly negative or feminine day, when the influence of Divine Mother is strong. If you try to force a different line of meditation, you will not get very far—you will feel frustrated. But if you become still in spirit, letting the picture quietly unfold, you will find yourself entering into a heavenly state of consciousness which may be either a 'sun' or a 'moon' state. We could well call the lovely sign of Cancer the sign of the infinite and eternal garden and the heavenly home, or the New Jerusalem, for here we realise the perfection of form in the heaven-world. We are in this garden; it unfolds to our inner vision, we have no need to create it—we are there, quite still, absorbing the beauty, the heavenly quality of the Divine Mother; or we may be in a gracious temple, or in the heavenly city—the New Jerusalem.

At this point, we are absolutely attuned to the guide of our spirit, the one charged to help us throughout our earthly life. Every soul has a spiritual guide or teacher to inspire and watch over them. If you are bereaved, it is here that you will feel close to your own loved one in spirit, whom you so long to contact.

On the positive days, the Sun–Leo days, when you come into the heart of the temple, you feel impelled to go to the altar where the flame is burning—the flame of the sun. You become one with the flame—you feel yourself rising with it into the heart of the sun—reaching up and out to infinity. You realise the meaning of the words, *I am in the Father, and the Father in me.* You are in a heavenly state of illumination and awareness of spirit from which you do not want to move. Nothing is impossible to this radiant sun–spirit—the Golden One—*You*, the real you.

Now the polar opposite of Cancer is Capricorn and that of Leo is Aquarius. Both are ruled by Saturn, the planet of steadfastness and concentration; the planet which stabilises, crystallises and creates a condition of permanence. When you have reached this point in meditation, you have built the etheric bridge into the heaven-world—the ladder down which the angels can come to minister to your spirit. Anything that happens now on the outer plane has ceased to disturb your meditation (except an extraordinary intrusion). No stray thoughts enter because this power of Saturn has steadied your concentration, and focused it entirely on the world within. You are in the garden, you are in the flame. Rest here—be at peace.

Now we come to the sixth and twelfth houses, Virgo and its polar opposite Pisces. These are the signs of health and healing, signs of the heavenly food, the bread and the wine. In this consciousness of the light we partake of heavenly communion; we receive healing. The dense particles of the etheric body which interpenetrates the physical body have become loosened and we are permeated by the light which heals, which relaxes, which enables us to feel that all is well.

Our consciousness continues to expand until we feel ourselves truly to be one with the universal Christ, the Grand Man of the heavens, who is represented by all the twelve signs. We realise how the Grand Man of the heavens is in us, and we in Him. So we understand the symbolism of Pisces—of the soul as a fish in the great ocean of cosmic life.

To touch this point in meditation is unforgettable. It

brings healing, and enables one to radiate healing to others. Pisces is the sign of the Great Healer, Jesus. How often, at the end of our meditation, we are guided to follow the Master into the healing temple to radiate the light to humanity!

Nonetheless, so long as we occupy a physical body, we have to come back to the physical consciousness. It is hard to return to the physical 'prison' after that lovely contact, but just as we need to exert the will to go into the inner world, so we must exert it to return. We come again to Libra, the exaltation sign of Saturn, and the sign of balance and equilibrium—the bridge between heaven and earth. Again we consciously make use of breathing, and firmly breathe ourselves back into the physical consciousness.

After being in deep meditation it is necessary to do this quite deliberately because at first one is deeply aware of the division between the two states of being. Returning to the physical life feels rather like getting into a box and closing the lid—but it is most important for the lid to be firmly closed, otherwise the physical and etheric bodies are not properly fused which can cause difficulties with health. In the White Eagle meditation groups, we follow a special routine which brings us firmly back to earth with every chakra well sealed.

'The leader of the group should say, "It is now time to return to the physical consciousness and to resume our responsibilities of the earthly life." After a pause the Lord's Prayer should be said in unison, and a benediction should follow. Then there should be a pause for silent thanksgiving; after which the leader should say: "And now we close down each individual centre of our being." We do this by an effort of will . . . and the following words are said . . . "We now mentally make the sign of the cross-within-the-circle upon each of our centres: on the crown of the head, on the brow, the throat, the heart, the spleen, the solar plexus and the kundalini [the base of the spine]." There should be a brief pause between the mention of each centre, which is thus closed and sealed by the Divine Will and the Power of the White Light of Christ. The meditation is concluded by each sitter *mentally* drawing a line of shining light round the outside of the aura of the body seven times. We do this by means of a sevenfold breath. We begin by drawing an imaginary white line, from the left foot up the left side of the boy, over the top of the head, down the right side and under the feet. As we start to draw the line up from the left foot we gently inhale and continue this *inbreath* until the top of the head is reached by the line of light; then we slowly *out-breathe* as the imaginary line is continued down the right side to join beneath the feet, thus completing a perfect oval of light which conforms to the shape of the aura and seals it.'*

When we realise that each of the chakras of psychic centres comes under the rule of a certain planet and opens the door to a different plane of consciousness, we understand even more how knowledge of esoteric astrology can help unveil spiritual truth. It is the science of religion the world over, which leads man to the understanding of the mysteries of his own being and of his unity with God and the universe.

---

* *Meditation*, pp. 31–3.

# Index

# THE WHITE EAGLE
# SCHOOL OF ASTROLOGY

Instruction in the White Eagle School of Astrology is by correspondence course, prepared by Joan Hodgson, and there are also regular meetings and lectures in London and in Liss, Hampshire. The three courses are designed to guide the student from the earliest stages to become a professionally qualified astrologer, and culminate in a Diploma examination.

## Beginners' Course

This starts from first principles and is so simple and clear that anyone with interest and determination can successfully calculate a chart and give a simple interpretation by the time they finish the twelfth and final lesson.

## Intermediate Course

For students who already know how to calculate a chart. These six lessons take such students to the point where they are ready for the advanced course in horoscope delineation.

## Advanced Course

The advanced course in horoscope delineation makes a thorough study of the interpretative side of astrology, including rectification, vocational guidance, chart comparison, health, karma, and the deeper spiritual aspects of the chart.

All necessary material is supplied with the lessons, and each student receives individual tuition. Further details of these lessons may be had from The White Eagle School of Astrology, New Lands, Liss, Hampshire, England GU33 7HY.